Quietly
COMES THE Buddha

Quietly COMES THE Buddha

Awakening Your Inner Buddha-Nature

ELIZABETH CLARE PROPHET

Inspired by Gautama Buddha

Introduction by KAREN Y. LeBEAU

SUMMIT UNIVERSITY PRESS®

QUIETLY COMES THE BUDDHA
Awakening Your Inner Buddha-Nature by Elizabeth Clare Prophet
Copyright © 1998 by Summit University Press. All rights reserved.

No part of this book may be used, reproduced or transmitted in any manner whatsoever without written permission, except by a reviewer who may quote brief passages in a review. For information, write to Summit University Press, P.O. Box 5000, Corwin Springs, Montana 59030-5000. Telephone 406-848-9200. Web site: http://www.tsl.org E-mail: tslinfo@tsl.org

Library of Congress Catalog Card Number: 76-28087
ISBN: 0-922729-40-9

SUMMIT UNIVERSITY ꞷ PRESS®
Summit University Press and ꞷ are registered trademarks.

Editorial and research: Karen Y. LeBeau
Interior design and production: Lynn M. Wilbert

Printed in the United States of America
First Printing 1998

Contents

Illustrations

Preface

I owe praise and gratitude to the *Lalitavistara* and *Jataka* stories of the past lives of the Buddha. It was my meditation on these texts that prepared me to receive the revelations from Gautama Buddha on the Ten Perfections for *Quietly Comes the Buddha*.

These are the original perfections that Gautama taught. They are eternal and they complement perfections adopted by later Buddhist schools.

The teachings in this book are written in the first person so that you can commune directly with the heart of this precious Buddha.

I dedicate this work and all of its merit

to the children of Tibet. May the Buddhas of

the Ten Directions keep these blessed ones safe

and happy and always mindful of their

magnificent heritage.

There is no path in the sky...
one must find the inner path.
All things indeed pass away,
but the Buddhas are forever in eternity.

GAUTAMA BUDDHA, *The Dhammapada*

Meeting the Buddha

You're wandering in an art museum, not really thinking about anything. The dial tone humming in your mind is interrupted by the resounding of your footsteps on the marble floor. A good interruption though, reminding you of your presence.

After all, it had been one of those mornings . . . Agreements that seemed solid as steel disintegrated into meaningless sawdust. Each phone ring signaled another disappointment. Another failure.

So you took a break and escaped into a museum. You're looking for solutions, but all you hear in your mind is a dial tone.

A multitude of paintings line the hallways, but none grab your attention. They blend into one another, colors blurring, unfocused. The dial tone hums . . .

Turning a corner you find yourself in the Asian art section.

Then it hits you.

Peace. Clarity of mind. Sweet stillness. Where is it coming from?

You focus on a gilded wooden statue in the center of the room. Moving closer, you see it's a seated man with short curly hair. His eyes are closed and he is smiling. The feeling of peace in your heart grows stronger...

"Who is this man," you wonder as you find the description placard. *"The Buddha in Meditation,"* it reads. *Buddha* means "awakened one" in Sanskrit. This man is enlightened.

The placard continues:

> The Buddha was born in 563 B.C. in the foothills of the Himalayas near the border of India and Nepal. He was a prince of the Shakya clan and was named Siddhartha. He left his family and kingdom to find the meaning of life. Siddhartha practiced austerities for years, but he still couldn't find inner peace. So he decided to take a more balanced approach through meditation.

Buddha. It echoes in your heart. Where have you heard that name before? In silence you study the image. Gentle cracks dispersed throughout the gold leaf betray its ancient origins. But the wood, so intricately and delicately carved, breathes with life. Organic. Pulsating. There's a presence in this relic.

Is it your imagination or is his smile broader than

before? The museum light above him flickers, then suddenly becomes brighter. Where have all the other people gone? It seems like hours since you've heard other footsteps through the halls. You're completely alone.

Your sense of peace intensifies and a comforting warmth suffuses your heart. Your open hands start to tingle, as if receiving a gentle mist from a light rain. Soon your whole being is enveloped in buoyant peace.

"Listen well," the Buddha speaks to your heart, "for I shall tell you how to become the Buddha where you are."

Whoa. You shake your head. This is only a statue, isn't it?

"The statue isn't the Buddha," he responds to your thoughts. "I am the Buddha. I can radiate my presence through the statue."

You shake yourself again, and convinced you need a cup of coffee and a serious reality check, you head for the exit. But a sign by the door catches your eye:

Buddhists use art to inspire and enhance their spiritual experiences. In Eastern tradition Gautama Buddha and other Buddhist deities convey their blessings and guidance through art. In Japan, for example, devotees have reported Buddhist statues coming to life to personally ease their pain and distress. One statue of the Future Buddha Maitreya is believed to be particularly skillful in healing eye, ear, nose and throat ailments as well as infertility and hardship with childbirth. Buddhists in China and Korea have recorded similar stories of divine intervention through sculpture and other Buddhist art.

You read and reread the sign. Suddenly the words tumble from the placard, rearranging themselves into scintillating echoes:

The Buddha is *here now*. He is always present. He speaks to his devotees unencumbered by time and space, be it in ancient India or the twenty-first century in the United States.

You turn and notice other Buddha statues in the room, each highlighted in a soft yellow glow. Slowly you step up to them and read: *"Dipamkara, the Ancient Lamplighter Buddha." "Maitreya, the Future Buddha." "Amitabha, the Meditation Buddha of Limitless Light."*

But your attention is drawn back to the center of the room. The gilded wooden statue shines brighter than them all. You walk up to him, gaze at his smiling face and again feel his loving presence.

"How can I become a Buddha," you ask. "I thought there was only one Buddha."

"There are many, many Buddhas," Gautama replies. "Don't you know, they're as numerous as the stars on a midsummer's night. And I, Gautama, the sage of the Shakya clan, am not the first Buddha, nor am I the last.

"You can become a Buddha because the very essence

of the Buddha is in your heart. This is the Buddha-nature, the potential to become a Buddha. All life contains this Buddha-essence. It's a seed. You can cultivate it and watch it grow. Or you can let it lie dormant.

"More than ever, all who are destined to become Buddhas must realize their Buddha-nature and fulfill their calling. The survival of Mother Earth and all sentient life depends on it."

Becoming a Buddha to save the earth, what a great idea! The last time you thought about becoming a super-being to help the planet was when you read Superman comic books as a kid. There he was, surveying the planet from outer space, figuring out who he'd save next. You liked that. So here is Gautama Buddha, a great enlightened being who wants to save the earth. But this isn't a comic book. This is for real.

"How did you, Gautama, become a Buddha?" you want to know. "How did you do it?"

"For me it all started when I experienced *bodhichitta,* my ardent desire for enlightenment. It ignited my inner divinity. That was my conversion, my turning around.

"*Bodhichitta* is the awakening of one's Buddha-nature. Without this initial *bodhichitta,* the Buddhas past, present and future could not have attained enlightenment.

"I am the Buddha for the current age, but aeons ago there was another Buddha named Dipamkara. At that time I was embodied as a young Brahmin named Sumedha.

I was successful and had accumulated much wealth. But after some time, I became bored with it all and wanted to find my true purpose in life. More than anything else in the world, I wanted enlightenment. It was an insatiable burning in my heart. That was my *bodhichitta*. So I gave away my wealth and possessions and became a hermit.

"Then I heard that Dipamkara was going to pass through the forest where I was meditating. So I joined the local people to prepare the road for him. Before I had finished clearing my part, I saw Dipamkara coming. I noticed that he was about to step into the mud. I didn't want him to get his feet dirty, so I laid myself down in the mud, offering my body as a carpet for this blessed Buddha.

"He was pleased and became aware of my heart's burning desire. With his Buddhic powers he could see countless ages into the future, and he prophesied that I would be a Buddha named Gautama. I rejoiced.

"So throughout many succeeding embodiments, I pursued and cultivated the qualities of a Buddha. You have also been preparing through a number of lifetimes. That's why you're here today. At this moment you don't remember. But you will.

"Yes, that description on the placard is right. I had been a prince. But like your Jesus in the West, I preferred a higher kingdom, not an earthly one.

"I was born in a beautiful garden. A few days later soothsayers predicted I would be either a great monarch or a Buddha. My mother, Maya, died right after that. Sadly, I never knew her. My father, Suddhodana, naturally wanted me to follow in his footsteps and become king. He did everything he could to keep me preoccupied with the pleasures and fascinations of worldly existence. But I had my own path to follow.

"My soul was starving and nothing in my father's palace could satiate me. I had been insulated from the world and I knew I had to get out to see it for myself. So I snuck out of the palace grounds four times.

"The first time I went out, I saw a decrepit man leaning on a staff. He was bald except for a few wisps of white hair. Brown splotches covered his skin. His face was deeply creviced. His eyes were sad, very sad, as he moved slowly, heaving with each studied step. He was old. Old. I couldn't believe it. Why hadn't anyone told me that people grow old!

"The second time I went out, I saw a man lying on the side of the road. Moaning, he braced himself on his arm, coughed up blood, then collapsed on the ground. I asked my charioteer what was the matter. He told me the man was deathly ill and probably would not last the night. How my people have been suffering from disease! And I did not know it. I did not know it."

You've seated yourself before the statue of Gautama, and looking up into the carefully carved face, you notice a tear welling up in his eye. It rolls down his cheek, catches a fold in his sleeve and glides off his fingertips to the marble floor, glistening under the museum lights.

"When I went out the third time, I saw a corpse. Gray and decomposing, its body had given way to the skull and bones that protruded through. It stank. Rodents fed off its flesh with utter disregard for the human life that had so recently occupied its form. This was death. My first experience with death.

"I became pensive. Dissatisfaction bored through my soul. Lifetime after lifetime all humanity suffers. Why? Is there no escape?

"On my fourth outing I was studying the throngs of people and thinking about their predicament when I noticed a man in a saffron robe. There was a feeling of peace about him as he made his way through the crowds. Somehow I knew he had found inner serenity.

"He was barefoot and clothed in a simple garment, but he looked more majestic than any monarch I had ever seen. 'Who is he?' I asked my charioteer. 'He's a wandering sage, a holy man, sire,' he responded.

"I looked down at my silken garments, splendid jewels and sandals. And I was ashamed. How shallow was my nobility as I stood before one who truly had integrity. I knew I could no longer be this prince.

"These four experiences stirred in me a soul memory. Do you know what it was?"

Shaking your head from side to side, you admit you don't know.

"It was a memory of taking my bodhisattva vows. I was a bodhisattva before I became the Buddha. I vowed to win enlightenment so I could save humanity. This was my promise to God. This was my *bodhichitta.*

"There are different types of bodhisattvas. Some bodhisattvas are celestial, like the Bodhisattva of Compassion, Avalokiteshvara, a powerful intercessor for those who cry out for mercy. Other bodhisattvas are earthly, like you. But each of us vows, above all, to set all sentient life free.

"From the very first moment your heart yearns to be a disciple of the Buddha, you have entered the bodhisattva path. This path is the training course on becoming a Buddha. You want to be fulfilled. You like to help people. You sense the urgency of redeeming the environment and upholding Mother Earth. What better way to accomplish these goals than by becoming a Buddha?"

The Buddha leans over and looks you straight in the eye.

"Listen. Buddhahood is not realized in a day. It's a ten-step program. You take on Buddhic qualities in increments. There are ten key virtues, or perfections, to this path. You can study them and incorporate them into your life. This was my prayer to cultivate these qualities:

Om, Buddhas of the Ten Directions,
May I fulfill all perfections:
Alms, precepts, renunciation,
Wisdom, courage, patience,

Truth, resolution, goodwill and indifference.
Grant that I may realize them fully
And attain supreme Buddhahood.

"These are the *paramitas,* the Ten Perfections, the precious qualities of a Buddha. They heal body, mind and soul. Each one is like a facet of a jewel, and when you enter into it, it reveals to you its secrets.

"So in numerous lifetimes I pursued these perfections. I studied and practiced them until I became one with them. But I could not attain these perfections through human desire. I had to purify myself of the human consciousness. I became transparent so that each precious quality could shine through me. And only then could the perfection become my own. That's how I became the Buddha.

"This noble goal of becoming a bodhisattva has always been a part of my teaching. But centuries after I left the physical earth, there were many misunderstandings about what I taught. Much of it had been forgotten and the spiritual thread of the Dharma was almost lost. Some schools clung to their misinterpretation of the rules. They even began to claim that only monks could pursue enlightenment. Can you imagine that?

"So I waited and searched for those whose hearts were prepared and opened. When they communed with me in meditation and prayer, I imparted to them a new understanding of the bodhisattva path, revealing that all sentient life possesses the Buddha-nature. Therefore anyone—a lay-man, laywoman, monk or nun—could become a Buddha.

"This was around the time of Christ, and the move-ment that developed from these revelations became known as *Mahayana,* which means 'great vehicle.' It's called the great vehicle because it welcomed everyone to the path of enlightenment.

"This movement ignited hearts throughout Asia, and that in turn inspired other new schools, such as Zen and Vajrayana Buddhism.

"You see, I have been imparting my teachings to select disciples throughout the world for twenty-five hundred years. And I continue to do so today.

"I can do this because I operate out of three intercon-nected levels of being. This is the idea of the Trikaya, or the three bodies of the Buddha—the Nirmanakaya, Sambho-gakaya and Dharmakaya. You have them too, latent in your Buddha-nature.

"The Nirmanakaya was the physical body I wore to convey my Buddhic presence and teach my followers when I walked the earth as Shakyamuni, the sage of the Shakyas. Otherwise, how could they perceive me and receive my teaching?

"In the body of my Higher Self, my Sambhogakaya, I convey my presence and teaching to bodhisattvas in the celestial realms. Those on earth who are spiritually developed can also commune with my Sambhogakaya consciousness.

The Three Bodies of Your Buddha-Nature
(Top to bottom: The Dharmakaya, Sambhogakaya and Nirmanakaya.)

"That is how I impart new teachings to uplift sentient life caught in samsara, the bitter sea of life. Certain souls receive my revelations, write them down and share them with others. This is how new schools were inspired.

"And my Dharmakaya, the body of ultimate reality, is the transcendent state of Buddhic essence. This is the Presence of the I AM THAT I AM."

The Buddha leans forward and cocks his head.

"You look puzzled. Do you have a question?"

Forgetting that the Buddha can read not only your body language but also your thoughts, you realize you've been distracted by conflicting concepts you learned in college.

You stand up to respond: "Yes, there's something I don't understand. Could you please explain why you use the word *soul?* I had a class in world religions—I think that's where I first heard your name—and the professor said that Buddhists don't believe in a soul. And what about God? My professor said Buddhists are agnostics, if not atheists. I don't get it."

Gautama smiles.

"Is your professor a Buddha?"

"No."

"Is she a bodhisattva?"

"I don't think so."

"Well, there you have it. Some people study Buddhism as a cerebral exercise, but they may not enter into the spirit of it—the bodhisattva path itself. So they can't penetrate or understand what truth really is. How can you describe water if you've never gotten wet? You don't need the human intellect to reach the mind of God.

"When I was Prince Siddhartha, many people believed that the soul was immortal. I rejected that but I did not deny that there was something like a soul, or lifestream, that continues to exist throughout the cycles of death and rebirth. Otherwise, what is it, then, that reincarnates lifetime after lifetime, making and receiving good and bad karma? What is it that experiences bliss and enlightenment?

"I use the word *soul* in a different way. The soul is one's potential. It can be molded, like clay. Because you have free will, you can shape the soul into the image of the Buddha. Or you can choose to produce a lesser image.

"So far as the Buddha being agnostic or atheistic, it's simply a matter of definition. If you say, 'God is an old white-bearded man who sits on a throne in heaven and torments his creation by hurling lightning bolts upon them,' then I will reply, 'In that case, I'm an atheist.' But if you say, 'God is a transcendent presence of love and wisdom who desires more than anything else to woo all creation back to his merciful heart,' then I will respond, 'Yes, I truly believe in God.'

"The Buddhas and bodhisattvas are individual manifestations of God. They are like points in a mandala or a complex geometric form. Though they are all part of the wholeness of God, each one is a distinct spiritual personality.

"They are not annihilated when they unite with God.

Their human consciousness is consumed, while their divinity, their Buddhic essence, is crystallized into permanent God-realization.

"God as ultimate reality, as the Adi-Buddha, extends himself in energy and form through a hierarchy of Buddhas and bodhisattvas. Through Tibetan Buddhism I revealed this hierarchy of Five Dhyani Buddhas, Meditation Buddhas, who are like step-down transformers for the Adi-Buddha.

"Each Dhyani Buddha receives creative essence from the Adi-Buddha and then conveys that enlightened consciousness to a Dhyani Bodhisattva. The Dhyani Bodhisattva, in turn, personifies that energy and creates in the physical world a *Manushi*, or incarnate human Buddha.

"There are families of Buddhas and bodhisattvas, you see. And many members of our families are on earth. We are one in transcendent essence.

"You, as a bodhisattva on earth, can become one with God. But how do you describe this union in human terms? Mystics throughout the world have had this problem. What words can communicate one's union with a transcendent, ineffable God? You can only resort to such terms as 'the void' or 'emptiness.' This union is the common thread, the common experience, underlying Sufi, Buddhist and Christian mysticism."

By now you're sitting on the floor before Gautama Buddha. You study his hands, his beautiful hands. In a graceful disciplined mode, they release a subtle essence from the center of the palms. You compare them with the hands of other Buddhist images around the room.

"How did you become the Buddha?" you ask again.

"After my four encounters outside the palace, I made the painful decision to leave my wife, Yashodhara, and my newborn son, Rahula. I loved them dearly, but the yearning for truth burned deeply in my soul. I had to leave. Their salvation and the salvation of the world depended on my finding the answer to human suffering. So I departed in the middle of the night, knowing that my father would take care of my beloved wife and son. I was only twenty-nine.

"I searched out the most advanced sages of the day, but none of them could teach me the secret of transcending old age, disease and death. So I went off on my own to practice austerities. 'Surely that will bring me enlightenment,' I thought. After six years I became weak from starvation and other self-imposed tortures. I nearly died. See?"

He points to a dark schist sculpture of an emaciated bodhisattva seated in meditation. The figure looks more like a skeleton than a human being.

"This statue is a reminder that going to extremes can be dangerous. So I stopped abusing myself. But what would I do next? How was I going to find the cure for human suffering? Not knowing my path to enlightenment, I almost despaired. Suddenly, I remembered an experience I had when I was seven years old.

"One beautiful spring day my father took me to an

Emaciated Buddha, schist sculpture, from 2nd to 3rd century A.D.
Gandhara, where the first images of the Buddha were created.
Gandhara included areas of current-day Pakistan and Afghanistan.
(Scala/Art Resource, New York)

earth-plowing festival. How joyous my people were in their
new tunics and flower garlands! After greeting everyone
and playing, I rested under a fragrant rose-apple tree and
watched them plow. There was something about the plow
blade penetrating the earth, then lifting its fertile, rich darkness to the surface. I fell into deep meditation. What peace!
What bliss! Even at that tender age, I realized that my experience was a taste of enlightenment.

"Recalling this gave me hope, so I pressed on with my

quest. I found a banyan tree and sat by its entwined trunks to meditate. Soon after, a woman named Sujata came and offered me rice porridge. She thought I was the tree deity! She had prayed to him for a son and promised him a special food offering if he interceded. Well, it so happened that she had just given birth to a baby boy, and in gratitude she brought me the offering. How fortuitous! That porridge strengthened me for my breakthrough meditation.

"I vowed I would stay under that tree until I achieved enlightenment. So I meditated all night. It wasn't easy. Mara, whose name means 'death,' tried to stop me. He sent his three voluptuous daughters to seduce me, but I was not moved. Then this evil one sent his armies to hurl hurricanes at me, a flood, flaming rocks, boiling mud and a storm of deadly weapons. Hordes of demons and total darkness engulfed me, but I refused to move from my seat.

"As a last resort, that audacious Mara challenged my right to pursue enlightenment and become a Buddha. He wanted my meditation seat. 'That seat belongs to me!' he shrieked. Mara called his retinue to witness that he was right, and his hosts of demons all shouted, 'We bear you witness!'

"I then called upon my witness, Mother Earth herself. For it was she who had inspired my meditative bliss when I was a little boy under the rose-apple tree. I tapped the earth with my right hand. In response, the earth quaked and thundered, 'I am your witness!' And Mara fled. With the obstacles cleared, my mind was opened to successive

Buddha in earth-touching mudra.
Contemporary bronze image in Nepalese style.

revelations through each watch of the night.

"The most important were the Four Noble Truths, which explain why humanity suffers so. The First Noble Truth is that life is suffering. When you are born, you suffer and your mother suffers. When you are ill, you suffer. You suffer as you grow old. And when you die, you suffer and others suffer in losing you. Throughout your life you suffer—you suffer when you experience the unpleasant. And then when you're having fun, you suffer because it has to end. You suffer when you don't get what you want.

"And do you know why you suffer so? It's because of desire. That's the Second Noble Truth. Suffering arises from inordinate desire. You want money, you want fame, you want power over others. Or maybe you just want to have a good time in the human experience. So what do you do to get these things? You ignore your inner needs, your spiritual needs, and you run around fulfilling all these desires and making a knot of karma. Then you die and have to come back to unravel it. It's all because you can't let go of your desires.

"It's a vicious cycle, but it doesn't have to be. And that brings us to the Third Noble Truth. If you want to stop suffering, if you want to heal your pain, then you have to stop entertaining inordinate desires.

"But it's not as simple as it sounds. Transcending desires of the lower self and its limited awareness is an ongoing process. You have to be patient and merciful with yourself. And you need guidelines, a path, to help you along. That's the Fourth Noble Truth.

"You can attain nirvana, liberation, by following the Noble Eightfold Path. It's the Middle Way, which strikes a balance between the life of pursuing pleasure and the path of severe asceticism.

"The Eightfold Path consists of: Right View, Right Motive or Mental Attitude, Right Speech, Right Action, Right Livelihood, Right Effort, Right Mindfulness and Right Contemplation.

"This is what I discovered as I meditated under the

Bodhi tree. I found the answers to all my questions, and more. And when I gazed at the morning star, I had fully become the Buddha, the Awakened One."

"Not bad for being only thirty-five years old," you quip. "But tell me, what were you meditating on when you discovered these truths?"

"Why, the Divine Mother, of course," the Buddha responds as he begins to intone in a low musical chant:

O Mother of the World,
We are all children of thy heart.
Kept apart by triviality,
We remain separate
From thy cosmic ecstasy.

Do thou now, great starry Mother,
Teach thy children how to have no other
Than thyself—to hold our hands from mortal error,
To keep our minds from mortal terror,
To seal our hearts in purpose now supreme,
To forge thy cosmic union—reality, God-dream.

Thy office of pure light fears no competition.
Let none doubt thee, but find instead
Attunement with thy blessed head
Of hallowed thoughts.

I am a child of cosmic diligence;
Immaculate is thy concept

> *Of my willingness to be God-taught,*
> *To learn to love,*
> *To shatter matrices of dense desire.*
> *O Cosmic Mother, from thy lofty star position,*
> *Set my heart afire!*

"I often taught in verse, you know. Look at the texts. First I gave the teaching in prose and then reiterated it in poetry. It was easier for my students to memorize the teaching through verse.

"After my enlightenment I began to preach. My first sermon on the Four Noble Truths became known as 'setting in motion the Wheel of the Law,' the law being the Buddhist teaching.

"I spent the rest of my life traveling and teaching. Many came to join me, and by and by we established a Sangha, a spiritual community. Eventually I returned to my father's kingdom to share my discoveries with my family. I rejoiced when my son, Rahula, and my beloved Yashodhara joined the Sangha.

"Ah, the Sangha. Such a precious jewel! When hearts come together in harmony and love, we can accomplish so much. We can heal one another and uplift sentient life. We can save a world..."

The Buddha's voice trails off as he turns his head and gazes upward. He looks like he's surveying another realm, some other horizon. So you keep silent and let him penetrate his moment. He sighs, then turns to you.

"How I love the Sangha. It is all that I lived for. The foundation of my path is the Sangha, the Dharma and the Buddha. These are the Three Jewels. Cherish them and take refuge in them.

"The Buddha is the anointed one who teaches, and the Dharma is the teaching itself, the spiritual law.

"But there's another meaning to the word *dharma*. It also means 'duty' or 'mission.' It's the divine law that can govern your life and lead you to freedom if you accept it.

"As the Buddha I release new teaching, Dharma. It is my duty to do so. Devotees in the Sangha receive and transmit the teaching. It is their duty to do so. As a result, more souls discover their Buddha-nature and join our community of bodhisattvas. And the Sangha above and below, in spirit and matter, expands. The Buddha, the Dharma and the Sangha represent the power of the three-times-three ever transcending itself. Profound mathematics, is it not?

"But bear in mind that there are always obstacles to overcome. It's not easy to bring spiritual light and principles into this terrestrial realm. The tools of Mara can take many forms to oppose you.

"My life was not always a gentle walk with my followers along the dusty roads and garden groves of India. I had to contend with my evil cousin, Devadatta. He wanted to destroy the Sangha from within, so he became a prominent member of the community. I lost five hundred monks because of his shenanigans. He even tried to kill me—three times!"

You stare at him in disbelief. You've never heard about such aggressive evil within a Buddhist community.

"How did you defend yourself?" you ask.

"I held my ground. I had been born into the warrior caste and was trained in the martial arts. Even so, I didn't fight him. I had learned a different way to deal with those who move against the Buddhic light.

"I dissolved his malintent by the loving power of the secret rays. I had cultivated these five Buddhic rays throughout aeons of embodiments. Each one has a feminine and masculine aspect—yin and yang, if you will.

"So in total I mastered ten qualities of the secret rays. These subtle essences are the *paramitas*, the Ten Perfections.

"I wasn't able to resent my cousin because I didn't have resentment in my consciousness. I was able to respond with loving peace because I had mastered the secret rays. These rays can penetrate the unconscious and subconscious to resolve psychological blocks to wholeness. I had learned a number of secret-ray exercises to attain self-mastery and inner power.

"One time Devadatta commanded the elephant keepers to loose a mad elephant. He was hoping it would trample me to death when I took my morning walk. Devadatta wanted to take over my position as the Buddha, you see.

People on the road were terrified when they saw the elephant coming. They fled, screaming. But I was not moved. I focused my attention deep within my heart, in the inner chamber of the secret rays. I was at peace.

"I raised my right hand in the pose known as the fearlessness mudra. Suddenly, five lions followed by five different-colored rays sprang out from my fingers. These Buddhic rays stopped the elephant dead in his tracks. He became docile.

"These are the subtle yet powerful energies you develop and refine on the bodhisattva path. These subtle emanations are inherent in all mystical teachings, but they may be interpreted in different ways. Taoists and martial artists understand them as ch'i, or internal power. Sufis call them 'essence' and the system of five *lataif*. Tibetan Buddhists describe this energy as emanations of the Five Dhyani Buddhas. I refer to them as the five secret rays.

"These secret rays emanate through subtle chakras in your hands, feet and spleen," he explains.

"You can see their different qualities depicted in the mudras of Buddhist and Hindu deities. Jesus also used his hands to convey the healing power of the secret rays.

"And there are secret-ray centers in each of the seven major chakras. The path to personal Christhood is refining within yourself the divine qualities of these chakras: wisdom, truth, power, love, peace, freedom and purity. When you have developed them to a certain degree, then you can enter the path to Buddhahood by cultivating the secret rays.

"Observe the secret rays being released through the mudras of the hands of the Buddhas and bodhisattvas."

You look around at the different statues of the Buddhas and bodhisattvas in the room. You notice that rays of light are beginning to shine through their palms and the tips of their fingers. You raise your hands to feel the energy.

"This indeed is like the ch'i I've felt practicing Chinese boxing," you reflect. "But it's a lot more powerful. So this is what my teacher Master Cheng meant by 'inner power.' It's the secret rays. He said inner power is a developed form of inner energy, or ch'i.

"Now I get it. These secret rays are the keys to my own healing and enlightenment, which I have been searching for all of my life. I bet they also provide keys for the healing of Mother Earth."

The Buddha smiles and nods at you.

"How do I learn more about these secret rays so I can become a Buddha?" you ask.

"Listen to me" the Buddha whispers...

CHAPTER 1

Becoming the Buddha

The seed of Buddhahood exists in every living being.
Therefore, for ever and anon, all that lives
Is endowed with the Essence of the Buddha....
It is immaculate by nature and unique with all,
And Buddhahood is the fruit of the seed.

UTTARATANTRA

Devotees Ever Mounting the Path of Attainment:

There are some who are born to be the Christ and there are some who are born to be the Buddha. Who is Christ? Who is Buddha? Who are you? Why were you born? To be man, to be woman, to be father, to be mother. Yes, this and more.

To be the Christ or to be the Buddha where you are, you must know that this is the goal of life for you. There are those who know from within, for their souls have cried out and they have heeded the call of conscience and inner flame. When you hear your soul cry out for deeper levels of fulfillment, listen and respond. Know in the inner recesses of your soul that life is meant to be a reflection of the infinity of God.

In the moment when your inner self and outer self merge, you realize that becoming the Christ or becoming the Buddha is the goal of life for all evolutions of beings in realms earthly and divine.

This is the moment when the spark of the Logos ignites the flame of the Buddha-nature deep within, and the all-consuming passion of the devotee becomes the search for the teacher and the teaching. Hence the vision of the goal inspires the soul to pursue the way of ultimate fulfillment.

Thus the Eightfold Path was born out of my communion with the Most High God—a communion that was a supreme compassion, a deep desire to show humanity how to return to the center of transcendent reality.

O flaming Presence of the Central Sun,
Spiritual source of all life,
O flaming Reality, thou Cosmic One,
O God, the All-in-all,
How can I impart the quickening, the awakening,
The awareness of the Enlightened One
To those here below?
They have forgotten the immortal fount—
Its taste, its soothing waters, its bliss.
Do they remember standing with Christ
On transfiguration's mount?
Do they remember beholding
The hand of God on Horeb's height
Or bearing witness to Elijah's flight?
Do they remember the kindness of your face
In bodhisattva's grace
Or in the shining eyes of arhat, adept, avatar?

To those who would return to thee
And yearn to glimpse eternity,
I would bring the light,
I would bring remembrance
Of the vastness of their origin.
I would bring a cup of living flame
From the altar of the Most High God.
I would offer the cup of liquid gold
To those who honor thee and would hold
Thy light, thy being
And the realization of thy law
In mind and heart and soul
That they might reach the goal.

I give my life, my energy
For the fusion of humanity
With sacred fire, with mind of God,
With love compelling and wisdom telling
That the way, the Eightfold Path,
Is the means of cycling
To the center of the sun
Of God consciousness.
The way made plain
Is for the humble in heart,
For they have prepared
To enter in.
The way made plain

Is the way of selflessness,
Desirelessness, all-inclusiveness.

I am the Buddha come again.
I am the Buddha come to win
Souls for freedom, for individuality,
Souls for God, for hierarchy—
Transcendent orders of Buddhas and bodhisattvas.
I am the Buddha.
I come quietly as all-pervasiveness,
As gentleness and sweet caress
Of God enfolding life with tenderness.
A thousand petals of a thousand-petaled rose
And of a lotus that blooms and grows
In the swampland of life
Is a symbol of the alchemy
Of dissolving karma
And transcending pain and suffering.

One by one the petals of the law
Will reveal a soul without flaw,
A jewel in the center of the lotus.
Enter the heart of Buddha-nature,
Of redemption's fires of Holy Spirit,
And welcome the initiation
And the process of extrication
To be purged of all illusion.
This is the testing and the tempering

Of a soul that is born to be
The Christ, the Buddha,
To be free.

I am the Buddha.
I come quietly.

Bidden by cosmic teachers, I come to tutor bodhisattvas East and West, to take you by the hand and lead you to Mount Everest. High in the Himalayas we shall stand, your hand in mine and mine in thine. We hold the hand of hierarchy.

So learn from me, if you will, of hierarchies of Buddhas and bodhisattvas, of worlds within and worlds beyond, of galaxies of light, of brothers and sisters you have known, now a part of cosmic consciousness. They know Shambhala, where the doves have flown.

The path of the Buddha is also the way of the Holy Spirit, of caduceus rising from the base to the crown[1] and fourfold mastery of planes of consciousness—etheric, mental, emotional and physical sheaths around the soul.

The way of the Buddha is the adoration of the Mother. It is the child adoring the Mother, the Mother adoring the child. It is God enveloping the soul and the soul enveloping God, the Lover and the beloved uniting as one. The way of the Buddha is the Knower becoming the known and the known becoming the Knower.

I would teach you of wholeness, of God as one and

God as twin flames, of God as three-in-one, as four, and on and on, until God as numberless numbers transcends all numbers and becomes the Infinite One. I would teach you to give birth again and again to realms of infinity, realms of God-realization.

I come that you might experience God as a Buddha experiences God. I come to prepare you so the Divine Mother can pass to you the torch of illumination, as I have entrusted it to her care. May you also transfer that torch of illumination, illumined action, and the experience of being God to all sentient life.

Enlightenment for this age is realizing the Buddha where you are. Let wisdom be the divining rod of love. Let your actions and experiences be reflections of all you have learned on the bodhisattva path. Prove the love of truth that reveals itself in eyes that shine for God and in a face transparent with the image of the Divine Mother smiling through.

Let enlightenment be upon souls who are free, free to win God-mastery. Let enlightenment be the mark of those who love and keep on loving still in the face of adversity and every thrust of tyrant's will. Let enlightenment be the love that consumes the poisonous dragon in his lair. This love is the rushing, crystal stream flowing on to a roaring waterfall of light, Iguaçu's torrents[2] drowning out the screaming and the screeching of the denizens of night from the unconscious mind. Let enlightenment be God's government on earth, God's vision on earth and God's victory on earth for a planet and a people.

I am the Buddha.
I come quietly.
Let the devotees of the Buddha listen well,
For I have a tale of attainment to tell.
Step by step I shall unfold
The glory of your becoming sevenfold—
Masters of the sacred law
And possessors of the forces ten.
Listen well, for I shall tell
The story of becoming
The Buddha where you are.

I am

Gautama

seated in the flame of peace

PRAYER FOR ONENESS
IN THE BUDDHA-NATURE

Om Buddha

Om Christos

Om Trikaya

*O Buddha, come forth to be thyself, myself,
as one. Awaken now the Buddha-nature within
me. Come now from out the great Central Sun,
focus of thy threefold light, threefold consciousness. Enter my heart and be the All-in-all as
universality, potentiality, realization, integration.*

*O Mother—wisdom of your heart, power of
your action, fire of your compassion—come forth
now. Precious jewel in the lotus of being.*

Om Mani Padme Hum

*Now I call to thee, great Buddhas—
Dipamkara, Gautama, Maitreya and Jesus.
Show me the way, the truth, the life everlasting.
Prepare me for the initiations of the heart that
I may become that jewel in the center of the lotus.*

Om Mani Padme Hum

Om Mani Padme Hum

Om Mani Padme Hum Hrih

⌒

CHAPTER 2

The Wheel of Perfection

Find joy in watchfulness;
guard well your mind.
Uplift yourself from your lower self,
even as an elephant draws himself
out of a muddy swamp.

THE DHAMMAPADA

Devotees Mounting the Wheel of Perfection:

The story of Sumedha is the story of a soul becoming the Buddha—your soul, my soul. In the course of myriad cycles of human incarnations, the soul begins to ponder the miseries of being caught in the wheel of rebirth and why it is subjected to birth and death, disease and decay. By and by the soul realizes that peripheral existence is vain, an endless chain of vanities.

After enduring more storms of sorrow, the soul reaches the point where it desires more than anything else to be free. At that point of conversion, of turning around, the soul makes a vow to return to its origins in God. Then the soul begins its journey to the center of the law and centers itself within the Flaming One. This is *bodhichitta*.

The way of the Buddha is the path of enlightenment through self-knowledge—knowledge of every aspect of the self, what the self is, what the self is not. The soul examines its succession of existences, of karma created by desire and seeking fulfillment through the physical senses. The soul yearns for something more than this, something within called eternal bliss. And when the soul is ready for the path of the Buddha, the Buddha comes quietly.

Humanity has sought escape, surcease from sorrow and freedom from the confines of the flesh. But few have sustained spiritual identity or secured their soul's destiny in perfection. When they seek only the answers to life in relativity, they imprison themselves in the laws of mortality. Self-made and self-imposed are these laws, and many have become a law unto themselves.

Ignoring the inner promptings of their soul's intuition, they wander through the labyrinthian caves of the subconscious and unconscious seeking reality. And Mara, in one of his guises, flatters and inflates their egos. He makes them feel special in a prideful way. Because of their distorted perception of the goal, they accept a counterfeit existence, insensitive to the misery of their soul.

To abide only in realms of the substrata of being ensnares the soul in nonexistence and in the way of death. Desire leading unto death and death unto desire becomes the oppressive twilight zone of mediocrity. It is a nebulous state of sin and struggle, neither light nor dark, good nor bad. And the soul is tortured, buffeted by returning karma, until it cries out for purification and liberation.

I come to clear the mental densities and to carve a

pathway from subterranean chambers unto the Himalayan heights. I penetrate the depths of the unconscious, realm of Homo sapien's thoughts and feelings, where Mara has enslaved humanity. I come with a light, a threefold light of the precious jewels—the Buddha, the Dharma and the Sangha. I come forth from nirvana, the Enlightened One, carrying the torch of the ages.

Let the souls who would be free find the way and follow me. As the Mother descends into the earth to claim her own, I also come to champion their identity in God.

I am the Buddha.
I come quietly.
And to all I now proclaim:
There is an escape from darkness unto light.
There is a way wherein the soul takes flight.
I point the way.
I am the way.
I am the Buddha of the light.

Now learn of me.
My way is clear
At Shambhala's threefold tier,
Flame-fountains pink, blue and gold,[1]
Tributes to the threefold flame—
God's heartbeat deep within.

Power, wisdom and love
Are the foundation of the law.

Tripartite light connecting hearts the world around
With the heart of God
Reveals the sacred mystery of my way.

Learn the balance of the Graces three,
Faith, Hope and Charity,
That consumes the hatred of the flesh,
Its lusts and endless infatuation
And self-perpetuation in illusory being.

As the candle of the lesser self
Is snuffed out in nirvana's grace,
So, too, its errors in mortality
Are swallowed up in God, immortality,
In the transcendence of the One.

And from the ashes of the former self
The phoenix of true self rises
In nobility, honor and purest love
Ignited by the threefold flame.
These three reveal the way of wisdom
And of wisdom's throne.

Let those who enter the sacred path
Affirm the victory of the light
And in Buddha's law delight.
For with every error you atone,
You free your soul
And raise a signpost for others to follow.

Let all secure my way,
The way of peace
And freedom in love's release.
Let all know this hour
That nirvana, as the consciousness of God,
Is attainable here and now.
Make your vow to selflessness
And seek the way of bliss
For freedom of all sentient life
In liberation's happiness.

Cultivate faith, hope and charity
In perfect balance three
And hear your soul's approbation
Echo in the temple of being:

There is a way.
God is the way.
There is escape from human consciousness.
God is the way.
I shall find the way and follow
Until I have become it.
And when I have found
Surcease from this mortal round,
I shall not take the leap,
The giant leap into the arms of God,
No, not yet.
For I must clear the way,

And beckon to humanity.
And set forth the law
By example without flaw
So the Buddha I would be,
So the Buddha I would see.

The path of attaining Buddhic light
Is the way of the Ten Perfections.
And when you've made each perfection your own,
Leave the reward of highest goal
And return to time and space
To fulfill your bodhisattva vow.

And what is this vow?
To hold the torch,
To lead those captive in ignorance
To the law of selfhood lived in God.
Compassion's vow
Is to anoint blinded eyes with the spittle
Until they see men as trees walking
And then the Buddha talking
And then the Christ upon the mount.
And when the blinded know their blindness,
They will be blind no more.
And when the stubborn and the willful
Kick no more against the pricks
Of their own karmic recompense,
They will embrace the Saviour on the way.

To fulfill that precious vow,
Experience blindness for a day—
Not the blindness of the cave
But the blinding light of the brave
Who dare remove themselves from Mara's toils
And starve the senses for a while.
And in that fast
They shed their false defenses
Of the nonexistence of the unreal self.
They cultivate the senses of the soul
And the sensitivity of the secret rays,
Expanding the soul like a rising sun.
They enter the whirling fiery center,
Solar consciousness,
And know God as shunyata, *the Cosmic Void.*

This is nirvana,
The realization of shunyata—
The place where God is real,
The store of energy whereby you heal
The wounds and war scars
Of these little ones.

Thus I say to all today
Who choose to walk my way,
Be prepared to take the torch of life
But not unto thyself.
The torch is for humanity,

And it is carried
By those who have extinguished
The candle of the lesser self.
Now let us see
Who will follow the Buddha
On the path of hierarchy.

In the center of the flame,
I am

Gautama

PRAYER TO THE
THREE JEWELS OF SHAMBHALA

Om to the sage, honor to the sage,
The great sage of the Shakya clan—
Tatyata Om Muni Muni Maha Muni
  Shakyamuniye Svaha!

Om Gautama Buddha,
Lead me to my inner Shambhala,
To the threefold light—
Faith, hope, charity;
To the precious jewels—
Buddha, Dharma, Sangha.

May I take refuge in them,
Tripartite light within
And the precious jewels
I seek in all who walk the earth.

O crystal of the mind of God,
O crystal of the mind of God,
Illumine me
And let thy mind be mine.

Lo, I am come to do thy will, O God!
Let thy fiat flow into the base chakra here below

And raise the fire from base to crown
That I may fulfill my vow.

Vairochana, come! Akshobhya, come!
Come, Ratnasambhava! Amitabha, come!
Amoghasiddhi, come! Come, Vajrasattva!
Enter with thy secret rays.
Come into the white-fire core
Of the Mother chakra,
  of the Mother's secret rays,

O Buddha, come! Gautama, come!
Tatyata Om Muni Muni Maha Muni
  Shakyamuniye Svaha!

꙳

MEDITATION FOR EXPANDING
THE LIGHT OF YOUR HEART

Although it is ideal to set aside time and space in a quiet place to meditate on the three-fold flame in your heart, you can use this meditation as a visualization at any point in the day.

Even in the midst of conflict, you can focus your attention deep within your heart. Visualize a tiny sphere of white fire. Feel this white light pulsate as it moves and scintillates in your heart.

Coming out of the top of this white sphere are tiny flames—blue to the left, yellow in the center and pink to the right. They are one sixteenth of an inch in height. But as you enter deeper meditation, they expand and grow as tall as you are.

See the three flames equal in height as they represent the spiritual qualities of God's power, wisdom and love in perfect balance within you. Visualize these flames beginning at a point beneath your feet and expanding until they are nine feet high.

Should you find that one flame seems smaller than the others, you'll need to cultivate the qualities of that flame until it is equal in height to the others.

Meditate in your heart of hearts and discern which of the flames of love, wisdom and power is the tallest and strongest and which is the smallest and weakest. Silently ask your inner Buddha what you need to do to bring these flames into balance. Listen for the answer...

Now turn your attention even deeper and listen to the heartbeat of God, to the heartbeat of the Buddha. Feel the love of the Buddha. It expands from your heart, from your threefold flame in ring upon ring of misty pink light.

See this mist dissolve the barriers to harmony. See it dissolve all hardness of heart within yourself and in those with whom you have had conflicts. See the conflict consumed in an intense blaze of pink, violet and ruby fire.

Now meditate on the peace of your soul's resolution in the heart of the Buddha. Visualize your threefold flame again and see it and yourself sealed in a sphere of white light.

⌒

CHAPTER 3

The Perfection of Alms

The essential nature of all Bodhisattvas
is a great loving heart, and all sentient beings
constitute the object of its love.

NAGARJUNA

Devotees Defining the Perfection of Alms:

Indeed, the story of Sumedha can be the story of your soul, of one who recognized the goal of Buddhahood, pursued it valiantly and won. Striving to become a Buddha begins with self-mastery formulated in the fiery core of being. Truly this is the light that lighteth every man and woman born of the essence of God. Those who apply themselves diligently to the bodhisattva path are not afraid to make a strenuous effort to vanquish the human will and declare "Peace, be still!" to the tempest of human emotions and the turbulence of the human intellect.

To enter Buddhic consciousness, to recognize within one's soul Buddhic initiation and to remember the ancient lineage of myriad Buddhas, you must have already prepared yourself.

In previous existences you have become familiar with the way of the cross and the fourteen stations of Christ consciousness.[1] The fourteen stations of the cross are initiations in the masculine and feminine energies of each of the seven rays. These are the rays of wisdom (yellow), truth (green), power (blue), love (pink), peace (purple and gold), freedom (violet) and purity (white). These Christic qualities correspond to the crown, third eye, throat, heart, solar plexus, seat-of-the-soul and base-of-the-spine chakras respectively.

Sumedha had learned the ancient way of Christ. And he had earned the right to recognize the Buddha, for he had forsaken the senses and the pretenses of the human consciousness. And thus the apertures of his soul, as chakra sensitivities, had been quickened and filled with light to master the seven rays.

To be the Christed One is to be anointed through self-discipline and to persevere through adversity. This is the foundation whereby the Christed Ones prepare to meet the Buddha in the way and receive his initiation in the Ten Perfections, the masculine and feminine qualities of the five secret rays.

Therefore, attain mastery in the seven rays. Come to Shambhala as victors bold, as masters of the flame. And by your humility you will recognize the conqueror, the Lord of All the World.

Sumedha—your own soul and mine—had resolved to find the path and to let nothing hold him back. And his heart was filled with joy when he heard that the Buddha Dipamkara was coming by the way. While Sumedha was clearing the path for the holy one of holies, he meditated on the Buddha's name, which means "kindler of lights."

Within his soul he did proclaim: "The Buddha comes!
All hail, the Buddha comes to reign!" He meditated upon
the law of the three and three, the six-pointed star of sacred
power that can save all sentient life.[2] And as he visualized
the image of the Buddha enthroned within his heart, lo,
came the Buddha Dipamkara.

The path was not yet cleared. Quickly he laid himself face
down upon the mud so the approaching Buddha and his disciples might walk over him. As Sumedha lay waiting for the
procession of the Buddha, he contemplated how he might discover the method to transmute corruption and become the Incorruptible One. And he pondered in his heart how he would
secure wisdom and all knowledge through Buddhahood.

With each yearning in his heart, each desiring to be
whole, the compassionate one earned the right to represent
the soul of humanity. For he sought omniscience not for
personal adulation in this world nor for personal gain in
worlds to come, but to help others cross the bitter sea and
reach the shore of sweet salvation. He sought enlightenment
to become a Buddha for humanity, a Buddha here and now.

The one who desires to become a Buddha must find
wholeness through humility so that all might walk over
the body of the Buddha, pass through his mind and be
nourished by his energy and self-mastery. The soul lying face
down in the mud, the soul determined on the path of selflessness to serve all sentient beings, vows that it must accomplish

this before taking leave of earth and entering into nirvana.

Then Dipamkara the Buddha stood before Sumedha prostrate in the mud and proclaimed to all that in vast cycles yet to be, Sumedha would be crowned a Buddha, Lord of All the World. The destiny proclaimed by Dipamkara that day was not only for Sumedha but for every living soul. The only difference between Sumedha and other souls was that he accepted his God-ordained destiny, his responsibility to become the Buddha.

Be like the soul of Sumedha and accept your future attainment and the presaging of that attainment in the ever-present now. Be that soul who seizes the fiat of the Lord of the World "Thou shalt be the Buddha!" with the vow "I am the Buddha here and now!"

It doesn't matter that in your present awareness you feel that Buddhic attainment is far away. Understand the opportunity you have been given and accept it. Prepare yourself line by line through the virtues of the wheel of perfection. For these virtues are flames of the one great flame, petals of the thousand-petaled lotus in the enlightened crown.

Don't wait for a Buddha or a Christed One to magically bestow upon you attainment. Determine to be the Buddha now and pursue with diligence the Ten Perfections. Then build the foundation of your Buddhahood gradually by increments of the secret rays. And one day your soul will find itself a veritable magnet of the Central Sun, magnetizing such Buddhic light to illumine bodhisattvas yet to be.

If you would be the Buddha with Sumedha, study the Perfection of Alms. It is the total giving of oneself, the continual emptying of the jar of water that the jar might be filled again. It is the self-emptying, the bestowing of the love of God freely to all.

This virtue is the testing of selflessness. For only souls who internalize the flame of selflessness can be trusted with the crystalline shafts of God's power. Only in selflessness can a soul be trusted with omnipotence.

When you receive a blessing from on high, convey it freely to all without the hindrances of the ego or expectations of adulation. Be like a crystal transmitting the light of the sun. Then God can bequeath to you limitless energy and the six sacred powers of the bodhisattva path.

Learn to give and learn to receive. Have faith that everything you give and all your good deeds shall return to you tenfold by the power of the Ten Perfections in the Wheel of the Law. Test this law, but have faith in it first. And even in the process of testing it, sustain your trust and faith.

You must realize the Perfection of Alms in your soul and in your etheric, mental, emotional and physical bodies. Meditate on your threefold flame and let it infuse these four lower bodies of fire, air, water and earth with the virtue of the Perfection of Alms.

Discernment and compassion must govern giving. The Perfection of Alms lies not in casting one's pearls before swine, nor is it the unwise use of gifts and talents that have been entrusted to your care by Buddhas and bodhisattvas, your spiritual overseers. For every morsel of Buddhic essence that is given must be well placed, secured within the heart chakra of both the giver and the receiver, then multiplied in grace.

Contemplate and meditate upon the Buddha within yourself as the giver of every perfect gift. And contemplate and meditate upon the Buddha within the receiver of your gift. Know that all givingness is to vest the self as God and then bestow this love of God upon all humanity here below.

Multiply the power, wisdom and love of your threefold flame by mastering the sacred elements in the body of the Mother. This is the sacred alchemy of immortality. See the layers upon layers of filigree that make up the bridal veil of the Queen Mother of the West, starry goddess of the Kunlun Mountains. Immortal one who bestows immortality, she merges with the Bodhisattva of Compassion—Avalokiteshvara, Kuan Yin, Chenresi—and becomes the Eternal Mother.[3]

See how the tripartite flame of Shambhala will give you the mastery of the Conqueror of the World over fire, air, water, earth. This is the mastery of the Buddha who pressed the four alms bowls into one.[4] Then see how the four vessels of temporary housing are but clay pitchers in this temporal world, tents we live in from dust to dust. And as we return again and again to the red dust earth, the bitter sea of samsara, we forget our origins in the Eternal Mother.

Throughout the ages she has sent her emissaries to remind us who we are and to help us return home. They have said, "Receive the sparks of *bodhichitta* and turn around. Let it impel the envelopes of the mind and the emotions to attach themselves to gossamer veils that carry our souls aloft to heaven's abode, the abode of the Eternal Mother."

Meditate on the nexus of the mind of Buddha, where sacred elements of consciousness converge. This is the point where the Buddha gives and receives from earthly bodhisattvas and earthly bodhisattvas receive and give to the Buddha.

So for many lifetimes Sumedha pursued the Perfection of Alms until he reached the quintessence of the law and gave his all, offering his life that others might live.

We remember the Christed One who said, "Except you eat the flesh of the Son of man and drink his blood, you have no life in you."[5] Therefore the ultimate giving of self is when the soul realizes that it must give itself as light to be assimilated by the body of humanity. In this giving, the candle of the lesser self is extinguished and the threefold light of real identity is ignited. This is the first step to nirvana.

I leave you with the contemplation of the first of the Ten Perfections. When your contemplation becomes unmitigated action, the Lord of the World will proclaim you the master of the Perfection of Alms and you will have begun the path of the Buddha.

I am waiting to receive you into the thousand-petaled lotus of my crown.

Buddha

THE TEN VOWS
OF THE BODHISATTVA OF MERCY

Om Avalokiteshvara,
I take refuge in thy mercy.
May I follow in your footsteps
And be compassionate to all.

O great Mother of Mercy,
Eternal Mother,
Kuan Yin, Kannon, Tara,
I embrace thy path
And the ten sacred vows:

May I quickly comprehend the entire Dharma
of wisdom and liberation.

May I soon attain the penetrating,
discerning eye of wisdom.

May I quickly save all sentient life.

May I soon attain upaya, *that power of love*
and compassion to be all things to all people
and lead them to enlightenment.

May I quickly board the prajna *boat and*
reach the shore of perfect wisdom.

May I soon transcend samsara, life's bitter sea
of suffering.

May I quickly attain the precepts, unwavering
meditation and the Tao of the Buddha.

May I soon ascend the mountain of nirvana.

May I quickly realize the unconditioned essence
of the Buddha.

May I soon be one with the Dharmakaya.

Om Namah Avalokiteshvara,
I take refuge in thy mercy.
Om Mani Padme Hum
Om

~

CHAPTER 4

The Prediction of Dipamkara

I rejoice at the Bodhisattvahood and at the
Buddhahood of those who have attained salvation....
The Buddhas and the Bodhisattvas are everywhere,
unimpeded and instantaneous.
All is in their presence.
I am standing before them.

SHANTIDEVA

*To Those Who Would Follow in the Footsteps
of Sumedha:*

    And so the Lord Dipamkara
    Prophesied the future
    Of the Buddha to be:
   "Behold the disciple of the Lord!
    Behold the devotee of the Word!
    Behold the one! Lo, he has come!
    The Tathagata,
    The Thus-Come One,[1]
    Sumedha in the world to be,
    A Buddha in the world shall be."

    He spoke of the great renunciation
    Of that one, Sumedha,
    And of his struggle fierce.
    He spoke of the austerities,

The sacrifices and compassion
Of that one, Sumedha,
Who would be known
As the Compassionate One.

And to all the multitudes
The Lord did proclaim
The future name
Of this beloved son,
Of his mother and his father,
Maya and Suddhodana,
And that name bequeathed to him,
Gautama,
Emanating from aeons vast,
From golden ages past,
From rings of light around the sun.

And from out that sun,
The I AM THAT I AM,
Would be born the soul
Of the Shakya clan.
Gautama is the celestial name translated
For the Buddha that would be the fire of God—
A flaming spirit
Descending like a rod,
A ray of divinity from heaven.
Gautama is his celestial name,
Gautama the name of sacred flame.

Dipamkara spoke
To all the people gathered there
Of events foretold
And the law of old
Written in the Book of Life.
He spoke of sons and daughters
Of prophets and kings
Who would come forth
In future time and space
To fulfill the Dharma
And resolve earthly karma.
They would intone the poetry of angel devas,
Giving praise to the elemental spirits,[2]
And they would sing with the gandharva musicians,[3]
Giving homage to the ancient Buddhas
And magnify the wisdom of the ages
For a new age to come.

So Dipamkara prophesied that this Son of sons,
This King of kings,
This Buddha of the Buddhas
Would come forth
To meditate beneath the banyan tree
And, tarrying there,
Receive the rice porridge
From the mother fair.

He would come to seek and find
The Golden River flowing,

To bathe therein,
To put on the adornment of the saints,
To form the pellets forty-nine
Of the rice porridge all refined,
To sustain him for each day of his nirvanic bliss,
Then to go the way,
The conqueror's way,
To the place of the tree of wisdom.

And Sumedha—
A soul fearless in the right,
A soul brilliant in the light,
The one of glory
Descending from the throne of grace—
Would take his place
Where every Buddha sits
From the beginning to the ending
Throughout aeons of cosmic destiny,
This sacred place for entering the heaven-world,
This place on earth
Consecrated by the Lord of lords.

Beneath the fig tree he would sit
In the place immutable,
Of the law irrevocable.
Here wisdom's fount and wisdom's throne
Nourished the Buddhas of the ages.
Here one day would Sumedha come
To face the East from the immortal Bodhi tree.[4]

And Dipamkara said:
"Here resolute in wisdom absolute,
One day in cycles yet to come,
This devotee,
Lying here before you
Face down upon the mud,
Will come to face
The cosmic consciousness of the One
And enlightenment procure.
Behold Sumedha, the Buddha of the future!"

Dipamkara also named five of the disciples of Gautama who would be initiated into the secret rays: Maudgalyayana, Shariputra, Ananda, Kshema and Utpalavarna. They would take their place in the mandala of the five-pointed star of

Ananda

Shariputra

Kshema

Maudgalyayana

Utpalavarna

mastery in the Ten Perfections—five points without, five points within.

As keepers of the flame, disciples Maudgalyayana and Shariputra imparted the mighty flow of wisdom here below. They held the threads of Buddhic consciousness and of the cosmos' web of life while draping worlds with crystal fire mist. And that cosmos, stretched upon the warp and woof of the creative mind, passed through the heart, the soul, the spirit and the chakras of a Buddha yet to be.

Then Dipamkara prophesied: "And Ananda, beloved cousin and disciple, must hold forth the third secret ray as a point of transition for the two chief disciples of the masculine secret rays, Maudgalyayana and Shariputra, and the two chief disciples of the feminine secret rays, Kshema and Utpalavarna. Then within the fiery core of the five-pointed star enthroned upon the throne of grace, Gautama will take his place holding the inner keys of the sacred mysteries."

When Dipamkara had spoken thus to mortals and immortals, he and his procession moved on, ever onward and upward in the Dharma and on the path of the Lord of All the World. Then Sumedha, archetype of humanity and Buddhic exemplar, slowly rose out of the mud. His soul rejoiced as he contemplated the magnificent path of self-mastery unto Buddhahood.

And from out the ten thousand worlds came the proclamations of the masters of the Ten Perfections and the Buddhas of the Ten Directions. And they affirmed the foreordained events and cosmic happenings—the melting of the elements, the raging of wind and water, and the quaking and the shaking of worlds within and worlds beyond. All these and many more were witnessed by the Buddhas of the ten thousand worlds, who did profess, "Of a certainty and of a truth, a Buddha of the future thou art."

Thus all the signs of the coming of the Buddha were fulfilled, for the soul of Sumedha had willed it so. He diligently pursued the Ten Perfections and embraced the quickening and chastening, the self-elevation and self-immolation.

And because Sumedha accepted the torch of Dipamkara that day, in future aeons yet unborn one called Gautama would hold the mastery sevenfold and enter the secret rays. He would become the epitome of the law, the sacred fire and the threefold flame.

Behold Sumedha, your soul and mine! Behold the Buddha-nature, the hope of all the world! Behold the Buddha of your soul!

I bow to the Buddha Dipamkara, to the abounding, unbounding Eternal One, precipitator of omnipotence, omniscience, omnipresence and the abundant life.

I am

Gautama

The Lord of All the World,
Holding the banner of Dipamkara

PRAYER OF THE BUDDHA TO BE

Om Buddha of the Light
Om Dipamkara
Om Tathagata
Ancient bearer of light, kindler of fire,
come forth!
    Enter now my soul. Enter, dear one.
Enfold me in thy flaming presence. Be my soul.
Come, make me whole!
    Clear me now by thy transfer of light.
Let me be the freedom of the light, the freedom
to free all life, all sentient beings, from unreality.
This is my prayer.
    I am the Buddha to be, the Buddha in
the world to come, proclaimed by Dipamkara.
I rise upon the fountain of the Mother light.
I rise to the heart to be thy light, to be the All.
    I am the Buddha. I will be the Buddha.
For the Lord has said, "Go, be the Buddha
where I am."
    Om Buddha of the Light
    Om Dipamkara
    Om Tathagata
    Om

MEDITATION:
The Golden Box of Resolution

Going within is the solution to finding
order for the chaos and problems of our every-
day lives. Before you begin this meditation,
think of a problem or obstacle that needs a
divine solution.

Going within means spiraling back in consciousness to the fiery core of your heart. Visualize this fiery spiral. It moves like a whirlpool
into the center of ultimate self-awareness.

Enter now into the center of this self-
awareness. Release your negative thoughts and
feelings into this spiral of light. When these
negative thoughts arise during your meditation,
let go of them and watch them dissolve in the
fiery core of love.

Focus your attention on your heart, deep
within the chamber of your heart. This is the
place where your Higher Self, your Buddhic self,
holds a vigil for you with such tenderness, such
profound understanding and such deep desire
to heal you.

See the particles of energy—thought energy,
emotional energy and even the energies of the

physical and etheric bodies—moving in a spiral toward the center of a galaxy superimposed over your being. See this galaxy as a fiery spiral infolding itself. Its flaming white-fire nucleus is in the center of your heart.

Now feel the energies of consciousness moving from outer sensation and outer awareness into this white-fire nucleus that is the point of reality of your Buddhic self.

Inside of this nucleus see the threefold flame burning and pulsating on the altar of your heart, even as it pulsates in the heart of the Buddha. Speak to the Buddha. He awaits. Whisper to his heart. Let him take from you all burdens. Accept his love and his intercession.

Become more and more concentrated within your heart. Visualize this Buddhic consciousness as a dazzling white-yellow sun now the size of a beach ball encompassing your heart and chest cavity. Allow the magnet of God's love, wisdom and power to draw you into the center of this sun in a beautiful natural flow, like a stream pouring into a gentle pool.

You are going home to your own Shangri-la. It's so close, so warm and so sacred. It's comfortable and welcoming.

When you look up into the heavens in awe of the stars and the celestial bodies, one star is brighter than the others. It is your star—your outer adoration becoming the blazing glory of your inner realization. This star becomes a celestial sphere suspended in spacelessness around your heart. And your heart is suspended in the timelessness of this star.

Behold a Buddha in the center of this sphere. You stand before him, place your hands together at your heart and bow. He smiles and gives you a glistening golden box. You hold the box to your heart with both hands, bow and withdraw.

Become aware again of the glowing sphere of light around your heart. See it enfolded and suffused with different hues of blue protection flame, expanding in rings to bless you and all sentient life.

Now open the box the Buddha placed in your hands and discover the divine solution to the problem you brought to this meditation.

ﮯ

CHAPTER 5

The Perfection of the Precepts

*The Tao has its reality and its signs
but is without action or form. You can
hand it down but you cannot receive it;
you get it but you cannot see it.
It is its own source, its own root....
It gave spirituality to the spirits and to God.
It gave birth to heaven and to earth....*

*The Big Dipper received it and from
ancient times it has never wavered. The Sun
and the Moon got it and from ancient times
have never rested.... The Yellow Emperor got
it and ascended to the cloudy heavens....*

*The Queen Mother of the West got it and
took her seat on the western mountain Shao-kuang—
nobody knows her beginning and nobody knows her end.*

CHUANG TZU

*Devotees Resolute in the Mastery
of the Ten Perfections:*

Sumedha was empowered by the Mother of the World[1] to cultivate the second perfection and all the precepts of the law. For he drank from the fount of her holy wisdom and received the fire of her love and determination.

He assimilated each precept facet by facet, absorbing the radiance of the diamond-shining mind of God. And by the alchemy of refining the Perfection of Alms, Sumedha resolved to invoke each point of wisdom in the mind of God as a sharpened arrow that would penetrate his mind and be assimilated. Then he would send that arrow back to the Creator's mind magnified by his understanding and gratitude.

Each arrow thus sharpened would penetrate layers of the human consciousness as well as levels of the mind of God, like a thread of wisdom connecting the mind of God to the mind of the spiritual seeker. And one day that thread would reach the center of God's creative mind and the soul would attain nirvana. This is the alchemy of realization.

There is a story in Buddhic lore about the yak cow and her flowing tail and her determination to protect her tail from being tattered or torn. She would stand unto the death if perchance that flowing tail were caught in the brambles or bushes, for nothing is more precious to the yak cow than her tail. This is the teaching of the Buddha of Buddhas: to guard and keep the precepts whole and holy. Guard them forevermore as the yak cow guards her tail.

For the yak cow's tail symbolizes the expanded energies of the *muladhara,* the Mother chakra. And these energies flow from the fount of wisdom of the Mother of the World, manifesting as the Goddess Kundalini herself,[2] deification of the white-fire coil of life in the base of being.

This is the fire of attainment whereby every Buddha does ascend the scale of being to enlightenment in the crown. This is the ladder of initiation from Omega to Alpha and Alpha to Omega.

So, then, the one who would walk the way of the Buddha must perfect these Ten Perfections and master the secret rays within and without. And each one of these five rays contains within itself the mastery of the Father, the active yang, and the mastery of the Mother, the passive yin, in the wholeness of the T'ai Chi.

Thus the Perfection of Alms is mastery in the divine masculine and the Perfection of the Precepts is mastery in the divine feminine. And these two comprise the test of our Father-Mother God in the first secret ray.

Throughout many lifetimes Sumedha fulfilled the precepts by meditating on the geometry of the One in the fiery core of being. Defining and refining this law of love, he cultivated the Perfection of the Precepts until he became known as the Keeper of the Precepts. For the law of the One, for the principle of precepts, he again laid down his life.

First he was assailed as the vessel of cosmic consciousness and of the divine memory of the gods. This was the test of fire and the etheric body. To attain the Perfection of Precepts, the brave Sumedha, soul of very souls, surrendered his body as the vessel of cosmic consciousness when he lay upon the soil in reverence for Dipamkara. And by the alchemy of air and the wind of the Holy Spirit in the precepts, he refined his mind. Moment by moment the soul of Sumedha internalized the sacred precepts. He proved the mind of God to be the mind of Buddha and the mind of a soul all in one.

And in the face of the raging of the fallen ones and of Mara and his armies, he proved the precepts as the mastery of water. He sat unmoved before the floods of Mara and withstood the pounding of the sea as he meditated on the mountain of the Queen Mother of the West.

The mastery of the earth and the alchemy of crystallizing salt is accomplished through the body of the Queen Mother.[3] This is the alchemy whereby Sumedha lay down his body to bear the weight of the Buddha and his retinue as he meditated on the secret rays. By this alchemy Christ bore the cross of the weight of world karma and was pierced through and through by the secret rays. Both souls remained steadfast in sublime contemplation on the God of very gods.

Sumedha kept the precepts to perfection, returning love for each affliction from the hordes of night, returning wisdom and the justice of God for each assault against the Shining One. Mara's senses were defenses—dense barriers built by fear and unforgiveness—against the Buddhic light. The Flaming One remained a flame, and those who sought to kill the body could not kill the flame. And thus, in the ultimate sacrifice, Sumedha anchored for eternity the golden flame of Buddhic light, the golden flame of the precepts of the law.

Chinese ivory carving of the Queen Mother of the West

So on that day, Sumedha, lying before the blessed Dipamkara, knew well what others failed to know. He confirmed the law: "This body that my soul does wear, 'tis good, 'tis good, expendable for the cause of Buddhahood. 'Tis better, then, that I renounce that which is impermanent ere the seasons turn and the Eternal claims what is not mine to claim. 'Tis better that I exchange the corruptible for the incorruptible and give to God and all sentient life what is only mine to give."

Thus, given the choice between the immortal flame and the mortal frame, Sumedha chose to seal the flame for humanity for eternity and to commend to God the vanity, the frailty of all mortality.

This is a choice
Every soul can make
In the here and now
And by transmutation's flame
Exchange the old man for the new.
For every soul can choose
To perpetuate the vow
To the perfections ten,
Dying to the old ways,
Living to the new
According to the precepts of the law.
To every soul determined to master
The Ten Perfections, I say
Pursue the precepts,
Pursue them without flaw.

I am

Gautama

in the immortal Buddhic flame

PRAYER:

The Alchemy of the Divine Mother

O soul, in the name of the I AM THAT I AM,
in the name of the Buddha, give thyself to God!
Fearlessly, courageously, empty thyself that thou
may be filled.
   O my soul, O every living soul, be God!
   By the light of Buddha and the Five Dhyani
Buddhas, come forth now!
   Om Vairochana Om
   Om Akshobhya Hum
   Om Ratnasambhava Tram
   Om Amitabha Hrih
   Om Amoghasiddhi Ah
   Om Vajrasattva Hum
   Mercy's flame, come forth in every soul
for liberation.
   Mercy's flame, come forth!
   O Queen Mother of the West,
   Goddess of universal alchemy,
   Prove the precepts within me
   That I may win immortality.
   Let the ocean of the Mother divine
   Sustain all sentient life.
   Om Mata, Shri Mata
   Om Mother, revered one,
   Embrace my soul!

⌒

CHAPTER 6

The Perfection of Renunciation

*After an arduous journey across the Himalayas,
a young seeker arrived at the cave of an old hermit.*

"Where are you going?" the hermit asked.

"To find Shambhala," the youth replied.

*"Ah! Well, then, you need not travel far," the hermit said.
"For the kingdom of Shambhala is within you."*

TIBETAN LEGEND

Devotees Seeking the Third Perfection of the Law:

The conditions and the conditioning
Of a Buddha to be
Comprise a symphony of cosmic majesty.
To perceive the Ten Perfections and their definition
*   and to refine and tune each perfection*
From deep within the soul
Even before there is a teacher to point the goal,
This is the challenge of a Buddha yet to be.

Therefore, O souls of my soul,
Humanity moving toward the central star of divinity
Carve out the Ten Perfections one by one
As a sculptor sculpts the face of God in stone.
This is not blasphemy.
It is to atone
For every error of the human race,

To seek the rod of divinity and to find
Line by line the measure of the law,
Line by line the face of God
Appearing in transcendent awe.

Therefore, O sculptor of the soul,
Take the blessed elements
Of air and fire and water,
And blend them into earth.
Carve there a soul of sacred worth.
And now let the soul,
The potential of the Buddha,
Be molded by the Potter.
Let it be filled with breath of life.
Let the creation strike forth
The note of the Creator.

Souls merging in the flame of Buddhic mastery,
Now tell me, I say,
Tell me the perfection of the three,
A bodhisattva's vows—
Renouncing the trappings of the world
To take refuge in the Buddha, the Dharma, the Sangha,
Renouncing enlightenment's peace to return and teach,
Renouncing nirvana's bliss until all life is free.

And as the perfection is reflected in the perfecter,
So tell me now, what is your vow?
Can you define the third perfection of the law?

Take a moment to meditate upon the fiery core of being, and see what the Lord thy God requires of thee.

And lo, Sumedha, your soul and mine, called forth from God the third perfection. He observed in awe the mandala of the saints and bodhisattvas who renounced all form and formlessness. He beheld their inner peace and saw how one by one they attained in wisdom and in the second secret ray through sacrifice, service and surrender.

He saw them gather into a spherical formation and began to meditate upon their mind. And penetrating deep into that mind, he transcended his human perceptions of the noble goal and surrendered his desire for it. He became one with God's essence, ineffable Cosmic Void. Realizing *shunyata*, emptiness, and the reason of the Logos, he attained enlightenment on this perfection.

The key to mastery, lo, I have found,
Is to view every mode and modification
Of this mortal round
As a prison house confining the soul
To illusion's veils in time and space,
In misery and in suffering.
So each saint and bodhisattva,
Subjectively perceiving the self
As a prisoner of the law of mortality,
Has one all-consuming longing—
To be free
From the forming

And the unforming of existence,
A prison house of clay.
Thus, in pursuing renunciation,
Look to God and to the sun within.
Renounce all else and thus thy victory win.

And so the soul of Sumedha wove a pattern of light through numberless rounds of existence in samsara until he fulfilled the perfection of self-abnegation. By surrendering the all, he attained the All. And meeting Mara on the way, as Christ too was tempted by the devil, he renounced the kingdoms of this world. He turned away from worldly honor and worldly acclaim. And in renouncing the kingdom and the desire thereof, he gained the kingdom within and the kingdom above.

The true kingdom is awareness of life's immortal bliss. It is self-knowledge of the higher ego. It is constant mindfulness of every facet of the soul. With the true kingdom of consciousness comes a greater defining of identity, a greater sense of selfhood and the strength of the divine self. The true kingdom comes when the Lord God crowns you with wisdom, wise dominion in the thousand-petaled lotus of the crown.

Those who would be great among you,
Let them be the servant of all.
Those who would be great among you,
Let them not serve the self

Nor fulfill any other desire save the desire to be
The Buddha for humanity.
Those who would be great among you,
Let them serve without attachment
Save the attachment to the law of individuality,
Without self-centeredness
Save the centering of the self in God.
This is the way of renunciation,
This is the way the soul of Sumedha trod.

And now there are footprints
In the sands of the Gobi Desert,
Once the Gobi Sea.
There is a path to Shambhala clearly marked.
Do you see?
Now let your heart burst forth
In poetry and song.
Now breathe a prayer
That every soul be free from wrong,
Free to pursue the path of right,
The Eightfold Path,
To the center of God-delight.

Here on the altar of Shambhala,
Enter now the threefold flame—
The flame of Christic renunciation,

The flame that is the fifteenth station[1]
After the way and the cross

And the fourteen aspects, yang and yin, of the seven rays.
'Tis the bodhisattva vow—
All merit to renounce
As compassion's sweetest offering,
Wisdom's penetrating gift
That the children might be free.

Come into the white-fire core,
That fire ablaze
With pink and blue and golden hue
And rainbow radiance of the creative mind.
Here in Shambhala come and find,
Come and find me in the center of the flame,
Where all who renounce
The modes of time and space
Live in eternity to reign.

I am in the lotus of Shambhala,
the Shambhala of your heart's desiring to be free.

Gautama

of the light

P R A Y E R :
Entering the Path of the Secret Rays

*O God, let me be all of thee as the Buddha
of desirelessness who transcends all desire.*

*Om shunyata, Cosmic Void of God being,
God cycling through my consciousness, my all,
my soul.*

*O God, I call thee now. Be unto me the
allness of the Greater Self. Consume the small-
ness of the lesser self. I would be the Buddha
where I am. I would be the Buddha. I would
quietly become the Buddha through entering
the path of the secret rays.*

 Secret rays, come forth now!
 Expand thy light through me.
 Bless and heal my four lower bodies.
 Illumine and raise
 My heart, my mind, my soul.
 Uplift the earth, our mother dear.
 Clear her elements
 Of all defilements
 That we may have a platform
 For Shambhala divine
 And free all sentient life.

     ↄ

MEDITATION ON THE DIVINE MOTHER KUAN YIN

It is a beautiful spring day as you walk near the temple square and enter a Chinese garden. The breeze carries a faint fragrance of lilacs blooming, reminding you to have hope in the qualities of mercy and loving-kindness.

You stroll along the flowery paths and stop at a number of shrines, each devoted to the Goddess of Mercy, Kuan Yin. You are blessed by her presence in each exquisite image of porcelain, wood and stone, all adorned with flower and fruit offerings.

You marvel at the subtlety of this sweet goddess and realize that the art of Kuan Yin truly touches the world in ways few will ever understand.

Soon you find yourself surrounded by lush pink, violet and purple lilacs. In the midst of them you come upon a Chinese maiden. She is dressed in flowing garments and carved jade adornments, and she carries a small golden vase covered with Chinese designs. She glows with love and compassion.

She is Kuan Yin, the Goddess of Mercy. She looks into your eyes like a mother lovingly looks into the eyes of her infant. You see yourself mirrored in Kuan Yin's heart flame, even as she is mirrored in yours.

Then Kuan Yin takes your hand as you walk along the footpaths. You whisper to her your burdens and concerns about loved ones near and far.

She turns and smiles at you, then lifts her vase above you, releasing pink-violet essence of mercy's flame, like a waterfall of flower petals that caress and enfold you. You feel peaceful, merciful love dissolving your cares and releasing divine solutions into your heart. You see your loved ones also receiving this waterfall of mercy's light. They are bathed in it, healed in it.

As you enter deeper levels of meditation on Kuan Yin's mercy, you see her larger than the planet itself. She lifts her vial of mercy above the earth and pours her loving compassion over all sentient life. This cascading mercy covers and penetrates the planet until it looks like a violet-pink sphere of gentle, peaceful light.

The earth is alive with the birth of spring and the resurrection, even while the coming of the Buddha and the Christ transforms the earth with their merciful love and their consummate peace.

ç

CHAPTER 7

The Perfection of Wisdom

Not knowing the way to the Temple
of Accumulated Fragrance,
I wandered through cloud-caught peaks
for several miles.
Amongst ancient forests and abandoned paths,
Where is the temple bell in these deep mountains?
A gurgling stream laps against lofty rocks,
The sun's hues pierce through teal pines.
Approaching twilight by the pool of Emptiness
I subdue the poisonous dragon through peaceful meditation.

WANG WEI

Devotees Searching for the Ten Perfections:

"Seek and ye shall find"
Is the fiat of the creative mind.
Seek and ye shall find,
O my soul, Sumedha,
Dwelling in the soul of humanity.
Sumedha, awaken to thy Buddha destiny!

When I attained the third perfection
And renunciation found,
I longed for soul fulfillment
As completion in this round
Of mastering the second secret ray
To coalesce into the second point
Of the five-pointed star of self-awareness.

Therefore, to wisdom's crown
I gave the all of my devotion—

To the crown of a Buddha yet to be,
The crown that one day
The Lord would place upon me
If I the Ten Perfections sought
And the battle with the serpent fought.

Meet the serpent mind
And defeat that mind
Using a warrior's strategy:
Position yourself
On higher ground in wisdom's crown
And transcend the enemy within.

This is the testing of the mettle of a soul,
The fourth perfection of the golden scroll,
Sifting, sifting grains of energy,
Separating by weight, measure and facet
Each nugget of gold, each diamond shining
In the crystal stream of energy
That springs from the fount of Reality.

Seize from God at his behest
And only by his command
The sacred fiery rod,
The scepter of authority.
And then go forth
To pounce upon the serpent in his lair
And plunge the rod of wisdom
Through and through.

Conquer the poisonous dragon at its inception
And replace it with the Christ-conception.
Expose the lie behind the serpent
Coiled inside the bag,
And free the devotee and the Brahman,
Supreme reality within,
From every woe and mortal foe
And all of illusion's boundaries—
This is the bravery of the soul.
To destroy the seed of Mara
That the seed of your Buddhahood might spring forth—
This is the test and the testing
Of the fourth perfection of the law.

Determined in the Perfection of Wisdom,
The soul, as precipitation
In Mother Earth,
Can now freely reign.
No longer shall the dragon stand
Between Divine Woman and her God;
No more can oppression divide
The lotus from the crown.
Now on earth as in heaven,
The fusion of caduceus fires
Flows freely as the river of life.
Father-Mother God, one in manifestation,
Prove the wisdom of the law of the Christed One,
The soul anointed to be Buddha in the way.

And so, expose the lie, my soul!
Expose the lie as energy coiled and entwined,
Like an overgrown bramble and vine
Choking off the life force of humanity.
And so, my soul, in wisdom know
The power of the Mother flow,
The Goddess Kundalini.
Invoke the upward spiraling energies
Of Mother Divinity.
And let the brambles and the briers
And all serpentine desires
Fall lifeless to the ground
To be consumed in sacred fires
Of the purity of the Mother.

Now, soul of souls,
To gain the wisdom of the Mother,
Seek her sacred energy
And determine to have no other.
Then thread by thread
Gather skeins of wisdom of the law.
Weave the seamless garment without flaw,
Protective sheath, a heavenly wreath
Around thy being.
And for the crowning glory
Of the crown of crowns,
Embroider lace of bridal veil,
A veil of purity to consume the veil of maya.

Seek wisdom as a holy oil,
As the blessing of the marriage
Of the soul to God.
This oil that anoints thy crown
Will release the fragrance
Of the thousand-petaled lotus
When the soul of a Buddha
Becomes the Buddha
In the power of the three-times-three.

Now these first four perfections of the law
Are for the mastery
Of the disciples of the Buddha
In the first and second secret rays
As one by one you take your place
In the mandala of saints and bodhisattvas.
May you fulfill your sacred vows
That all the children
And the sons and daughters of light
Might also give their sacred energies
To the Perfection of Alms, of Precepts,
Of Renunciation and of Wisdom.

And now let souls come forth
Who would carry the flame of Ananda,
Whose name means bliss.
He is the chosen one who carries the fires of transition
And the waters of discerning wisdom

That empower the bodhisattvas
And the saints to mock
The armies of the evil one.
And as keepers of the light
Of Buddha, Dharma and Sangha,
The bodhisattvas hold the torch
For those who would now cross
The bitter sea of time and space.
They would enter the sacred place
Where virgin consciousness does transcend
The errors of the human race
Unwittingly committed in ignorance
Against the Mother of the World.

Now let the banner of the Buddha be unfurled
As Ananda comes forth to teach
The way of the fifth perfection and the sixth—
The way of courage and of patience,
The way whereby the yang forces
Become the yin
And the fusion of the Father-Mother God
Gives birth to Buddhic awareness
In the chosen disciple of the Lord of the World.

I am Gautama.
I come to rule.
I am the Buddha
Born within the heart of humanity,

Carrying souls striving for the Buddhic light
To the place where God dwells
In Himalayan heights.
There I am enshrining the crown of the Buddha
As the crown of life for all
Who will master the Ten Perfections.
Will you mount the path
And claim my every footstep as your own
And then the pinnacle of perfection in the law,
The crown of five stars
Waiting at the summit?

I am

Gautama

In the silence of the highest peak
Of the highest mountain in the world.

PRAYER TO THE
MOTHER OF THE WORLD

The Mother of the World has ordained:
"Winds, gather ye! Snows, gather ye! Birds, hold
ye back! Beasts, stand ye back!

"No human foot shall set its traces on my
summit. The audacity of the dark ones shall not
surmount! The light of the moon shall not
endure! But the sun rays shall touch the peak.

"Sun, guard my summit, because where else
shall I keep my vigil? Never shall beast ascend,
nor shall human power prevail!"

Herself, the Mother of all Being, shall keep
her vigil with a fiery shield. What glows upon the
summit? Why have the whirlwinds assembled
a resplendent crown?

She, the Great Mother, alone ascended the
summit. And none shall follow her.

Upon the highest summit stands effulgent
the Mother of the World. She came forth to smite
the darkness. Why are the enemies fallen? And
whither do they turn their eyes in desperation?
She has cloaked herself in a fiery mantle and

encircled herself in a fiery wall. She is our citadel
and our striving.

   "The mountain of the Mother extends from
the earth to the heavens!

   "The mountain of the Mother extends from
the earth to the heavens!

   "The mountain of the Mother extends from
the earth to the heavens!"[1]

❧

CHAPTER 8

The Perfection of Courage

*Despite the emphasis on compassion
the Bodhisattva is no mere sentimentalist....
He is the Great Hero, the embodiment not
only of Wisdom and Compassion,
but also of* virya *or Vigor....*

*This aspect of the Bodhisattva's personality is
prominent in the well known Ahicchatra image
of Maitreya, with its powerful torso, massive yet
graceful limbs.... The right hand is raised palm facing
outwards and fingers slightly curved in the symbolical
gesture of bestowing fearlessness.*

BHIKSHU SANGHARAKSHITA

To All Who Would Walk in the Way of Courage:

Courage is the sign of the coming of age of the heart. The heart that loves knows no fear. For the heart that abides in perfect love has cast out every fear and the torment thereof.

Listen to the lion roaring on the horizon of the desert. Listen to the lioness roaring from the depths of the emerald jungle. Hearts spontaneous in fierce compassion to protect their own—who dares defy their presence?

So, lionhearted one, sound the roar of the bodhisattva! Declare your *simhanada*[1]: "Before Abraham was, I am!" And it is so.

Affirm your worthiness of Buddhahood, rising *bodhichitta* and compassion wrathful and tender. Transcend the limitations of time and space and receive the blessings of the Buddhas past, present and future.

Courage is for the mastery of the third secret ray, the

ray of excellence in the alchemy of realization. It demands of the Buddhic one perpetual mindfulness multiplied by the power of ten. Thus courage and patience go hand in hand as spirals of yang and yin dance and merge in Tao.

And so, my friends, let us study together that which makes courage, that which makes patience. By these you can master the secret rays and find the reward of going within to the white-fire core.

Courage is watchfulness. It is the heart that is cognizant of the All, the heart that by intuition is aware of every infringement upon the All. Those who keep the watch as watchmen on the wall of life must have the courage to defend the threefold flame in the secret chamber of the heart.[2] And the watchman who walks upon the wall of the Lord must be prepared for every foe and the beating of the war drums of the ego from the pits of the unconscious. For this is where Mara's emissaries wait to taunt and tempt the guardian of the heart.

To be the watchman is to be the lonely one. Do not despair in aloneness, for it is truly all-oneness with the presence of God. Be the keeper of the gate of awareness in Buddha and Christ, and guard the tender souls aborning in the womb of the Eternal Mother, souls eager to be born. As knight champions of old who came to guard the fold and to seek the chalice of the Lord, come one, come all who desire to become the Buddha. Come to defend the age of self-mastery.

Courage endures the night, overcoming the greatest of

all foes, which is fear, and the ally of fear, which is doubt. When the two entwine, they come disguised as ghosts of the mist to trip you up. They masquerade in masks of human deception, like the masks of Mardi Gras. They question and taunt you and make you feel that you should be like them. Do not give in to their macabre gyrations and intimidations by which they try to submerge you in fear and unreality. Summon your courage and roar! Be as fierce as the lions protecting their cubs.

And so, you see, since the fall of the fallen angels, denizens of darkness have moved against the soul of God. They project their fear and trembling in the hours of darkness, in the hours of the moon, to take from gentle souls the gift of the dawn. This gift is the comfort and presence of the Mother, reborn day by day as the fulfillment of her love.

Therefore, when you hear the cry, "Watchman, what of the night?" let your answer be: "All is well! All is well! For God is whole and I am whole. And in that perfect harmony I take the rod of power, the scepter of authority, and mark upon the sand the circle of our oneness. And I declare, they shall not pass! They shall not enter here! Nay, they shall not defile the virgin consciousness of immaculate wisdom. I am the watchman on the wall of life."

Now you see, keepers of the flame of life, how the enemy sends waves of fear even while you are winning, even while you are reaching the crest of victory's light. For when all else is lost, the enemy will inundate souls of light with tidal waves of fear. Thus the enemy seeks to win the battle of life by convincing you through fear to give up and lose hope.

Take heart, I say! Have courage in the threefold flame. Claim the light of Shambhala, the heart of Buddha where you are. The fires of courage burst forth from Shambhala, the heart of a planet. So be the heart of life where you are— the heart of family, loved ones and friends, the heart of community, the heart of a nation.

Let your heart resound with the roar of the lion. For the lion symbolizes attainment of the heart and the one who bears the essence of courage. Be that one who encourages all who walk along the pilgrim's way and says: "Fear not, for I am with you. Have courage. Be of good cheer, for I am the flame of love, wisdom and power ever near."

Courage is engaging your energy with alacrity, fastidiousness to detail, a keen sense of timing and an utter awareness of space hallowed by the presence of the Holy Spirit and the Tao. Courage is determination and a fiery will, seasoned by wisdom and nurtured in the Mother's love.

The greatest victories of all time have been won through the flame of courage allied with integrity and honor. Courage is the mark of those who have willed to win and vowed to defend the Mother flame embodiment after embodiment. On every front, in every city where bodhisattvas converge and work together for the victory, there the eagles gather as forces of light drawn by the universal body of the Buddha. And they overpower the venomous dragons, who come with their fire and smoke, breathing upon those who bear the ancient light of Dipamkara.

Be strengthened by the *virya*[3] of the bodhisattva and draw your swords of living flame. Let the rapier thrust of your sacred Word be the fire that proceeds out of the mouth of the two witnesses—the Buddha of your spirit and the Mother of your soul.

Call forth the invincible wisdom and compassion of Kuan Yin's jeweled ax, bow and arrow, shield and sword.[4] Intone her mantra Om Mani Padme Hum and subdue the enemies of Shambhala, past, present and future.

Thousand Hands, Thousand Eyes, Dynamically All-Pervasive
Great Compassionate Heart Kuan Yin.
Chinese woodblock illustration of the Bodhisattva of Mercy.

Take courage, take courage, O hearts of fire! Proclaim your victory! Proclaim the light of God that never fails. Stand before the tribunal of the world and speak the truth, and see how truth will set you free.

I rejoice to behold you in the white fire of integrity and honor. For it is a blessing, a sheath of courage from cosmic beings and the Elohim, the 'Divine Us' of our Father-Mother God. For you are the conquering hero, and you will taste the sweet elixir of victory as you become one with God through the perfection of courage. And when you experience the fruit of courage, determination, forbearance and a steady moving tempo marching into the light of the sun of God within your soul, you will never ever be defeated again.

May your heart be sealed in the flame of courage. And may you dissolve all errors of the past in the dazzling golden white light of the courage of the heart—the heart fired in adversity, the heart sealed in the diamond of God's love.

To the victors of courage belong the spoils of the human consciousness—the misqualified energies of the human race that are transmuted in the flame of purity. In that alchemy of transformation, the purified energies are returned to the victor as a gift of sacred life. And all the saints and bodhisattvas joyfully give to the victor their momentums of accrued merit, for they know that one will use them to free all sentient beings.

Thus, in the nexus of the heart of courage, the energies of humanity are purified in the crystal stream of God. And through that heart, the power of I AM THAT I AM radiates and heals all. Jesus Christ, the Galilean avatar and noble Son, had also attained this heart of courage when he proclaimed, "All power is given unto me in heaven and in earth."[5]

Therefore, O my soul—soul of Sumedha, soul of humanity on the path of divinity—purify the heart, the sacred chamber. Expand it wide and long. Increase its height, breadth and depth. And when the way is made clear, welcome the presence of Dipamkara. Welcome the Buddha, the Lord of lords, the conqueror on the way. Welcome the Lord of All the World into your heart, into the flame of honor, courage and integrity.

See how God dwells within the chamber of your heart. See how the white light swirls to the pulse of Shambhala, the Shambhala in your heart of courage.

I am the Buddha in the heart of humanity.
Summon now your divinity.

Gautama

P R A Y E R :

Intercession of Infinite Light

Om Buddhas past, present and future,
Om Maitreya, Initiator and Buddha
*   of the New Age,*
Enfold my heart in thy infinite light.
I bow to your infinite light.

Infinite light!
Shine now in the cave of being,
Fill me completely with light!

Infinite light!
Let shadows stand out, loom largely,
And fade quickly at the blasts of light from thee!

Infinite light!
I am one with Maitreya and the Buddhic light.
All darkness flees before this holy light!

Infinite light!
Flee, lust! Flee, greed! Flee, jealousy! Flee, hatred!
Flee, selfishness! Flee, laziness! Flee, unkindness!
Flee, all hurts! Flee, all wounds!
Flee, every thought that is less than light!

Flee, every feeling that is less than light!
Flee, every motive that is less than light!
Flee, every word and deed that is less than light!

Om Maitreya
Om Buddhas past, present and future
I am thy infinite light!
Om

SNOWBALL MEDITATION
TO CLEAR THE
FOUR LOWER BODIES OF BEING

When we strive to live the bodhisattva path, we can sometimes feel overwhelmed by our vows and the magnitude of the task. So we have to keep our spiritual perspective and know that with God all things are possible and then turn to the unfailing Buddha-nature in our heart.

Begin by visualizing a Buddha meditating within your heart. Feel the golden rings of peace and wisdom he radiates.

Bow before him and ask for help to overcome obstacles. (You can name specific situations.) He smiles and raises his hands in circular mudras to direct and coalesce all energy of life into the nucleus of the atom of self. Feel this action within and realize that this is your microcosm of being.

Enter the nucleus of this compressed concentration of light in your heart as though you were stepping into a translucent mother-of-pearl globe. You feel comfortable in this realm, which is teeming with life and the wonder of God.

In the center of this realm, you find a beautiful ruby and pink throne. Gently sit down on this throne and begin the next level of your meditation.

Focus on the fiery ruby and pink lotus of

your heart. Feel its warmth, and delight in the intricate beauty and fragrance of this divine lotus flower. In the center of the lotus is a beautiful crystal jewel reflecting light and all colors of the rainbow.

Through the transcendent, impersonal eye of your Buddha-nature in the center of the lotus, observe the results of your past actions. Survey pockets of inharmony and confusion that you have been caught up in and the resulting negative karma you have made through your four lower bodies—etheric, mental, emotional and physical. This karma looks like dust, cobwebs and debris cluttering up the home of your soul.

From your divine perspective you understand that these four lower bodies are chambers of consciousness. Visualize them as four levels of a house. The physical body corresponds to the basement and the foundation. The emotional body relates to the family activities that take place on the ground floor. The mental body indicates your contemplation and the activities of your mind in the study on the second floor. And the etheric body, in the upper rooms or the attic, represents the records of the past and the blueprint for your future.

One body blends into the next as the steps of initiation going up the spiral staircase take you from the basement to the skylight. When you reach the skylight, the rays of the sun reveal the shining pathway that leads back to the center, the secret chamber of your heart.

In this chamber you see a circular stairway to the stars fashioned out of the threefold flame, the sacred fire that translates the human consciousness into the divine. Standing on the stairs examining the house where the soul will abide for a time, you see cobwebs in the corners of the attic and the rooms, collections of odds and ends, photographs and scrapbooks—a coup d'oeil of the personality and psychology of the members of the household.

You see the records of family life in all of its happiness, moments of grief and strife, and the working out of ever-present karma. You also see the impediments to each one's Buddhahood. Chagrined by the negativity that has transpired in this place, you say to yourself, "What this house needs is spiritual cleansing and transformation."

Now in your meditation, project to every corner of your house, to every nook and cranny *light! light! light!* You are like a child throwing snowballs, up and down, to the right, to the left. You are flinging spheres of light into every corner of the house, to every level of your four lower bodies. The bursting balls of snow, as golden star-fire light, illumine and transform it all. Fling your snowballs of light at the pockets of negative karma, and see them dissolve in joy and forgiveness.

Hurl these golden snowballs of purity into patterns of unkindness and destructive habits. Fling them into that self-deception, which stifles every intuition of the heart and the gentle proddings of the soul's creativity. Then see the rooms sparkling clean and glowing with light.

Now you can redecorate and infuse new life into your home. Arrange objects of art and paintings. Transform the rooms with greenery, flowers and spiritual shrines. Fill your library with ancient tomes of spiritual wisdom, teachings on the angels and the Buddhas. And adorn the hearth where the flame burns perpetually in memory of Dipamkara Buddha, who rekindled by his own threefold flame the life of a planet and all sentient life.

Basking in the light of the threefold flame, create a vision of your four lower bodies as a living Shambhala, a living temple to the Buddha and the Christ consciousness.

As you hold this vision of perfection, recognize that in the oneness of the flame you are the transforming power, wisdom, and love of this home, which has now become your spiritual retreat.

✐

CHAPTER 9

The Perfection of Patience

Without patience nothing can be achieved....
Very often people give up a brilliant beginning
only because of lack of patience. They forget that
all great tasks are accompanied by difficulties.

HELENA ROERICH

To All Who Would Enter Communion
with the Bodhisattvas:

Just as courage is the sign of the coming of age of the heart, so patience is the sign of the coming of age of the soul. And patience is the understanding of the bodhisattvas. It is the long-suffering of those who, above all, would harmonize the light of the soul with cosmic law.

Those whose essence is *bodhi* and compassion[1] have the patience to endure all things until the law of cycles is fulfilled. Through mercy and the mastery of the five secret rays, they come into alignment with the inner blueprint of life and return to the white-fire core of being.

The patience of the saints and bodhisattvas is refined through trial and tribulation and through the testing of their souls in measures of loving discipline. There will be times— mark my words, devotees of the Buddhic light—when you will be required to stand fast against the hurricane of Mara's plane.

So you will stand upon the rock of Christ and cling to the tree of life. Then when the fierce wind and the storm, violent in its vituperation, unleashes the black magic of Mara against your soul, you will stand firmly in the place where the Buddha stood to proclaim the law. In that hour of trial remember the Bo tree, and let your refuge and your strength come from God on high. For God has set his seal upon you to be the Buddha of the law.

In order to pass the test of the ten and of the five secret rays, you must know that you are God. You are God in actuality, God in manifestation, God in every aspect of your expression.

But it is not enough to know you are God, you must become the Creator in the creation. You must render unto God the things that belong to God. Every organ in your body is a focal point for the release of God's light. Every cell and every system in the physical temple is designed to be the instrument for the fusion of God's energy into the physical dimension.

You must know that God lives in your heart as the threefold flame of Shambhala's light. You must know that God is the seed identity of your soul. You must know that God is a sun blazing in every chakra. And you must understand that even the physical organs are instruments of God's expression.

When you declare, "I AM THAT I AM," you must not exclude the body temple. Therefore, let God be your brain as well as your mind. Let God be your physical heart as well as the spiritual chamber therein. Let God be your eyes, your nose, your mouth. Let God be your lungs and your liver, your kidneys and your gallbladder. And understand, if you will, that every part of you that God has made is an instrument for the incarnation of the law.

Think not that this is a desecration. For I tell you that if you would be the body of God upon earth, you must seal every part of your body in light daily through prayer and visualization, mantras and contemplation. And when you call forth the protection of Archangel Michael and the Loka-pala guardian deities,[2] you must see the physical body as well as the spiritual complement of your whole being charged with blue-white lightning. See this light flushing out the physical toxins and the poisons that seep from the unconscious and attach themselves to molecules of light, causing disintegration, old age, disease and death.

When I went forth from my father's house, I saw for the first time the evidence of mortality—the plight of decrepi-tude, a diseased body, the lingering of death. I understood how these three imprison the flame of being and I felt the power of God welling up from within my soul. I heard the fiat of my own inner Buddha declaring the truth of being from deep within:

I am the life everlasting.
I am the life expanding without limit.

I am the life overcoming sin, disease and death.
I am the glory of the law
And the glory of the victory.
I am the Word incarnate.
Make me free, make me free,
Make me free, O Siddhartha!

I heard the call. I heard the compelling of the Logos. And the fire burned within my heart and soul and mind.

I saw the mists of maya. I saw the temptations of Mara. And I knew that I must take my stand unflinchingly, unceasingly, determinedly. For humanity must be free from the stain of sin and the sordid aspects of selfishness. Humanity must know the law.

In order for humanity to know that law, I must become that law through and through. I must not exclude the body, for the body is the Mother. I must not allow the forces of disintegration to attach themselves to my body temple or any part of it. I must wield the sword of the Mother to defend truth in every atom and molecule of matter.

By thus proving that God himself can and shall dwell in the tabernacle of matter, I would prove for all eternity for all evolutions descending into this vale of tears that there is a way out. And that way begins with the flushing-out of all debris and discord of the human consciousness. That flushing-out can be brought about by invocation to the flame and by following the path of the masters of the Far East.

For only the flame of God blazing, blazing in every plane of consciousness has the power to consume all wrong and to right every desecration of the Divine Mother.

I am the Buddha of the law. I am patiently waiting for souls of God to become aware of their inner vows to bear one another's burden and to carry a balanced burden on both shoulders. To the right is the weight of personal karma and to the left is the weight of planetary karma.

Thus I wait for the anointed ones to possess their souls in the patience of the fulfillment of the law. This is the great call of the Buddhas of the ages, the call to come into communion with them and their mandala of bodhisattvas and cosmic beings.

Come and wash your garments in the crystal flowing stream of the Mother chakra. Dip into the Ganges, and know that God can purify, God can sanctify, God can make holy even the muddied waters of the great river of life. And in the patience of the fulfillment of the law, God can also sanctify the bread and the wine as the Body and Blood of the Lord Christ.

Devotees of the Buddha, look up and live in the light! For miracles are happening every day. Remember the miracle of finding a four-leaf clover. Remember the joy of picking that four-leaf clover and knowing that the law of God in nature was proof that life is good.

The miracle of the three-leaf clover is the miracle of the threefold flame, the sacred trinity of Brahma, Vishnu and Shiva.[3] Saint Patrick taught this to the good people of Ireland as the trinity of Father, Son and Holy Ghost. Maitreya taught this to his disciple Asanga as the Trikaya, the three bodies of the Buddha.[4]

Now understand that when you have found the four-leaf clover, you have found the Mother. And the fourth leaf is for the crystallization of the God-flame in the earth. It is for the amplification of the light. It is the purity of the Mother that releases the power of the Father, the wisdom of the Son and the love of the Spirit most holy.

This is the miracle of life, that the saints and bodhisattvas in their patience await the coming of the Mother to bring wholeness into manifestation. They endure the return of karma, every astrological aspect and every erg of energy they have set in motion. They receive into their four lower bodies personal and planetary karma. And they draw into the fiery vortex of their hearts all energies requiring transmutation while enduring all that the law requires to fulfill the promise of the coming of the Mother.

Run to greet her on the path of life. Strew the flowers gathered in the fields. Strew them along the path to welcome the Mother. See the little children picking flowers for her coming. Hear them sing as they form bouquets of devotion to the Mother:

Mother, dear Mother,
I love thee, I do.
Praise be unto heaven
For the gift of you.

Your smiling presence,
Sweet essence from above,
Bearing resemblance to
An angel of love.

I shall be brave
When surrounded by fear.
How can I ever fail
When thou art so near me?
Mother, O Mother,
Let thy light shine!
Come to bless with happiness,
Angel divine.
I will give my all at thy call—
My life is thine.

Run to greet the Mother as she comes along the path. See her in the distance descending the mountain, over the hills and into the valleys. She comes to gather her children. She comes to receive them one and all into her arms of love.

The Mother comes without discrimination to nurture her children. All children are her own. She sees no flaw among them. To her each child is a precious flower of the Father-Mother God. And her love for God makes every child born of his heart a flower in her bouquet of praise.

When you greet the Mother, give her the flowers you have picked. For she will take them gladly and joyously to her heart. She will place them upon the altar of the Buddha as a gift of the children to their Divine Father.

The Mother is the mediator of the flow from the Father in spirit to the children in matter and from the children back to the Father. She is the intercessor of his great wisdom and conveys back to him the children's incomparable innocence.

To have and to hold the gift of the Mother is worth the exercise of patience. Therefore, patiently, patiently invoke the transmutation of all that she requires of you. For with every step upon the ladder of Buddhic initiation, you approach her fiery center, the womb of the Starry Mother, and enter the initiation of the five secret rays.

Patiently search for the four-leaf clover. Patiently pick the wildflowers in the fields of life. And receive both the tempest and the calm as the sign of the coming of the Lord and the turning of the Wheel of the Law.

Receive the fruits of all planes of existence into the fire of the heart for the glorious consummation of Father and Mother divine within the center of being.

I am, in the patience of the law, the Buddha forever.

Gautama

THE PRAYER OF
SAINT FRANCIS OF ASSISI

Lord,
Make me an instrument of thy peace.
Where there is hatred let me sow love;
Where there is injury, pardon;
Where there is doubt, faith;
Where there is despair, hope;
Where there is darkness, light; and
Where there is sadness, joy.

O Divine Master,
Grant that I may not so much
Seek to be consoled as to console,
To be understood as to understand,
To be loved as to love.
For it is in giving that we receive,
It is in pardoning that we are pardoned, and
It is in dying that we are born to eternal life.

CHAPTER 10

The Buddha
and the Mother

There is a beginning to heaven and earth
Known as the Mother of the World.
Once you find the Mother
Then you will know her children.
Once you know her children
You return to preserve the Mother
And abide in safety even after the body perishes.

LAO TZU

To All Who Would Be United in the Love
of the Buddha and the Mother:

Courage and patience are the twin flames of our Father-
Mother God in the white-fire core of the third secret ray.

Understand that courage is the thrust of diamond light
from Vajrasattva, the guardian of the secrets of the Buddhas.[1]
Courage sweeps the planet round with the intensity of God's
will through the mantra Om Ah Hum Vajra Guru Padma
Siddhi Hum, the Golden Mantra that neutralizes all chaos
and despair.[2]

Behold the stupa with its wisdom eyes gazing from each
facet.[3] Behold the beacon of the all-seeing eye radiating from
the lighthouse window. They reveal the way of victory to
souls East and West on the path of Buddhic initiation.

Courage is the crown of the Absolute and the measure
of the soul's wisdom wherein it becomes the patience of the
Mother. This patience is like the ringing of a ritual bell that

is prompting us to be mindful of energies in motion, emotion. These energies are the pulsations of the sun shining in her strength in the solar plexus, the rays of the Starry Virgin shining upon the just and the unjust.

Courage is the wisdom of the soul and the quiet knowing that all sentient beings shall be made whole when the Mother completes her meditation on the inner perfection of each one. This is the immaculate conception of the patience of the Mother. Perfect wisdom is her work and it shall manifest on the day of the Tathagata's appearing, the Buddhanature realized in each of her children.

The Mother is calm because she is the master of the science of the immaculate conception. By her immaculate vision she guards the consciousness and the seed atom of the divine masculine and the divine feminine. She guards the blueprint and the fiery embryo of Buddhic consciousness forever aborning in time and space.

And in guarding the all-seeing eye and the vision of perfection for every child, the Mother holds the reins of power, wisdom and love. Within her patient heart she sings a love song to the Buddha and rejoices in their union as she gives birth to man and woman made in the image and likeness of the I AM THAT I AM.

Patience is the virtue whereby the saints do magnify the Lord. Thus the feminine light within each one becomes the complement divine of the law of inner being.

Patience is purity waiting for each initiation, keeping the

vigil of the wise virgins and the light of the seven chakras and the eighth, the secret chamber of the heart. Let patience have its perfect work, fortifying and expanding the light of the chakras for the reunion of our Father-Mother God.

And so my soul, Sumedha, heard the call of courage—the coming of age of the heart—and he answered. He acquired the fifth perfection of the law through the mastery of water and energies in motion in the bitter sea of his own subconscious.

Jesus stilled the tempest with his "Peace, be still!"[4] and cured the disciples of their dreadful fright. So in the midst of a stormy sea, where all were affrighted unto the death, I also entered the heart of God's peace and found the key to the perfection of courage. My soul pressed on in the dead of night, mastering the raging seas as I pursued the promise of Buddhahood in a world to be.

Likewise, souls mastering the perfections in the twenty-first century must come to grips with the threatenings of life's storms. For these are the return of planetary karma and humanity's misuse of the energies of the Mother flow. Thus the world is being inundated by the records of the Dead Sea and the Gobi Sea and the blackness of their own misqualified energy.

Let the devotees of the Buddha and those who have claimed the way of Sumedha as their own now summon the *vajra* of the Father and the Father's thrust. Let them now sound the bell tone of the Mother and the Mother's trust.[5]

Hurl the lightning into the depths and dispel the fog

of ignorance. Bear with equanimity the hypocrisy and the pettiness of those who are the instruments of your initiation in the sixth perfection of the law.

To endure suffering is a virtue. But you must adjudicate the cycles and discern when to be the instrument of change and to call forth God's justice. Know that when you summon courage, patience will follow with her perfect work. And as you sustain this patience, the courage in the secret rays effects the change—altering molecules and atoms, dispelling misconceptions and confusion and laying the foundation for a new day.

Therefore, fulfill all that the great law requires of you. And demand answer from the Buddha as you pray for courage. May this courage you invoke consume by fire any suffering that is superfluous to your attainment of the Ten Perfections of the Law.

Understand, too, that the gift of the wisdom and the instruction you receive is from my own heart. This is the comfort of the Spirit in the days of tribulation when the bodhisattvas are required to endure all things. For those who endure unto the end of cycles, they shall transcend the toils of the wicked, the temptations of Mara and the negativity of their own returning karma. For love is the gift of patience.

Love is kind and envies no one.
It is never boastful, nor conceited, nor rude.
Love is never selfish and is slow to take offense.
It keeps no score of wrongs nor does it gloat over others' sins—

Love delights in truth instead.
There is nothing that love cannot face.
There is no limit to its faith, hope and endurance.[6]

Indeed, souls must cultivate loving patience, for they will be weighed in the great scales of the Buddha. And those who in love endure temptation and persecution for righteousness sake shall receive the crown of life that the Lord Buddha has promised them.

I dwell upon this initiation of the third secret ray so that you might understand that it is for the entwining of the flames of the Buddha and the Mother within your own heart.

And when you find no other explanation, no other consolation for the sorrow and the suffering that for a little while precedes the overcoming and the rejoicing, look to God on high. Look to the Lord Dipamkara and to his disciple Sumedha. Look to the soul within and hear the voice of hierarchies echoing from the central sun of life:

"I am the Lord thy God visiting the temple of being, testing the mettle of the soul. Unto that soul who has yearned and prayed for initiation, I release the opportunity to enter into the unity of the One. Now the soul can attain this unity by retracing those cycles that, although nobly begun, have ended in failure for want of consecration and putting down the temptation of self-preservation.

"Extinguish the candle of the lesser self before it scorches the garment of the Christed One to be and the Buddha on the path of golden immortality. Extinguish the candle of the lesser self. Leave it not to burn on in the night, for it could mar the filigreed veil of the Cosmic Virgin.

"I come with the energies of Kali, fierce mother and consort of Shiva,[7] to flail the arrogance of the dying ego, the beast that riseth up out of the sea and the beast that cometh up out of the earth. For these would destroy your sacred alchemy, the alchemy of the union of your soul with God. This is the goal of life in heaven and in earth. In the detail of the law, discipline thy vanity, O bodhisattva! Become Sumedha, soul of souls, and know that you are worthy to embody sacred light for all humanity."

Let the shavings from the little child's soap carving of the image of the Buddha be a sign to parents and teachers who would instruct these precious souls in the Dharma. For you must be the example to these little ones. If you would prove to souls that the light of God never fails, you must shave away the density, the indulgences and the narcissism of the personality cult. For these are perpetuated through the interchange of senseless conversation, sensual vibration, ego argumentation and the exaltation of the human personality at the expense of the divine.

Look not for human personality in the devotees of the Mother but for charisma of soul and the quietness of the Buddha. For those who follow the Eightfold Path know the Buddha within the heart and the quietude of communion with the heart of God, the heart of Christ and the heart of humanity.

So in patience possess the soul. Be sensitive to shifting states of energy and control the lines of force. Receive the light of the Creator in your four lower bodies, just as a four-leaf clover receives the rain and sun of the Mother and the Buddha.

Patience is the holding-on to the reins of the omnipotence of God in heaven and in earth. Patience is tenacity, the willingness to wait all night and day for the coming of the Mother and the Buddha. You cannot know the hour of their coming into your heart. Therefore, in the patience of the bodhisattvas, in the courage of the righteous, in the wisdom of the masters, tarry ye till we come.

Tarry in the New Jerusalem, tarry in Shambhala, Shangri-la. Tarry in the bowl of the chakras and in the secret chamber of the heart. And while you tarry, let your energy flow be the thrust of the Buddha and the receiving of the oncoming light by the wave of the Mother's love.

I am the Buddha in adoration of the Mother flame within you. Raise up now that Mother flame that I might behold the object of my adoring.

Gautama Buddha

PRAYER FOR
THE KINDLING OF TRUTH

*Life of my life, I shall ever try to keep
my body pure, knowing that Your living touch
is upon all my limbs.*

*I shall ever try to keep all untruths from
my thoughts, knowing that You are that truth
which has kindled the light of reason in my
mind.*

*I shall ever try to drive all evils away from
my heart and keep my love in flower, knowing
that You have Your seat in the inmost shrine
of my heart.*

*It shall be my endeavor to reveal You in my
actions, knowing it is Your power that gives me
strength to act.*[8]

RABINDRANATH TAGORE

MEDITATION AND MANTRAS
FOR DEVELOPING THE CHAKRAS

We can clear obstacles to our happiness and fulfillment by purifying and expanding the light in our chakras.

When we receive light from our Dharmakaya and 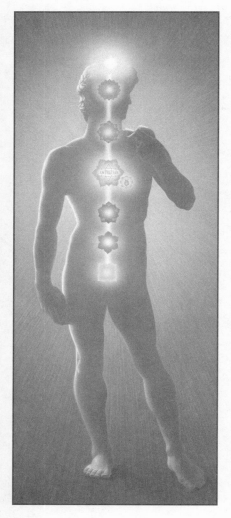 Sambhogakaya, it first enters the vessel of our heart chakra. This chamber is the place where the soul's efforts on earth are consecrated by the fires of the heart.

So when you meditate on each of your chakras, also be mindful of your heart chakra. You can hold the thumb and index finger of your left hand together and touch them to your heart when you want to enhance this meditation or whenever you feel the need to be centered in your heart.

Each chakra has a specific God-quality and bija, or seed syllable, mantra. As you visualize each chakra, meditate on its qualities while you intone the corresponding mantras.

The Crown Chakra

Visualize the crown chakra as a golden-yellow lotus with a thousand petals. Contemplate the Buddhic wisdom of the crown as you give the following mantras:

For purifying and balancing energies: *Om*
For protection and perfection:
    Om Aim Hrim Shrim Klim Sou Hu Om
For expanding the light: *Om*

The Third-Eye Chakra

Visualize the third-eye chakra as an emerald green lotus with ninety-six petals. Contemplate its qualities of truth, healing and single-eyed divine vision.

For purifying and balancing energies: *Om Namaha*
For protection and perfection: *Om Krim Namaha*
For expanding the light: *Shrim*

The Throat Chakra

Visualize the throat chakra as an electric sapphire lotus with sixteen petals. Contemplate its qualities of divine will, power and the spiritual blueprint for all sacred endeavors.

For purifying and balancing energies: *Om Ham Namaha*
For protection and perfection: *Om Sou Hu Namaha*
For expanding the light: *Sou Hu*

The Heart Chakra

Visualize your heart chakra as a pink lotus with twelve petals. Contemplate its quality of divine love.

For purifying and balancing energies: *Om Yam Namaha*
For protection and perfection:
    Om Aim Hrim Klim Chamundaye Viche
For expanding the light: *Klim*

The Solar-Plexus Chakra

Visualize the solar-plexus chakra as a purple and gold lotus with ten petals. See it highlighted with flecks of ruby fire. Contemplate its qualities of peace, selflessness and God's energies in motion, emotion.

For purifying and balancing energies:
Om Ram Namaha
For protection and perfection: *Om Shrim Namaha*
For expanding the light: *Hrim*

The Seat-of-the-Soul Chakra

Visualize the seat-of-the-soul chakra as a violet lotus with six petals. Contemplate its sacred qualities of freedom, compassion and forgiveness.

For purifying and balancing energies:
Om Vam Namaha
For protection and perfection: *Om Hrim Namaha*
For expanding the light: *Gloum*

The Base-of-the-Spine Chakra

The base-of-the-spine chakra is the chakra of the Divine Mother. Visualize it as a white-fire lotus with four petals. Contemplate the qualities of purity and harmony and the primal essence of Mother life.

For purifying and balancing energies:
Om Aim Namaha
For protection and perfection: *Om Aim Namaha*
For expanding the light: *Aim*

CHAPTER 11

The Perfection of Truth

The pursuit of Truth is true bhakti *(devotion).*
It is the path that leads to God, and therefore there
is no place in it for cowardice, no place for defeat.
It is the talisman by which death itself
becomes the portal to life eternal.

MAHATMA GANDHI

*Bodhisattvas Embracing the Life
of Crystalline Integrity:*

Truth is the seventh perfection of the law. It is the crystal flowing stream of enlightened consciousness. Truth is freedom. It frees souls from the bane of errors that they often commit unknowingly.

If you love truth, be willing to challenge unreality. Cultivate discernment and then you will perceive clearly what is true and what is not. To be a pillar of truth here and now, begin to self-reflect as you stand at the nexus of the cross of spirit and matter. Observe the workings of your mind and your behavior, and admit to yourself the right and the wrong of every thought, word and deed.

Let us not prevaricate. Let us not equivocate. But let us place our faith squarely upon the foundation of truth. For truth is an invincible shield, the armor of the Lord and the bulwark of the virtue of our Father-Mother God.

Truth is the perfection of the I AM THAT I AM. It is the boundless compassion of the bodhisattvas of the Diamond Heart.[1] Truth is the understanding of the penetrating soul who strives to become one with the Absolute.

Claim the truth of your immaculate conception, that you were conceived in perfection. For you were immaculately conceived in the mind of the Buddha and in the heart of the Eternal Mother. Know your identity in the Mother and the Buddha. This is your right and your duty.

Now let Prajnaparamita teach her children transcendent wisdom[2] that they may sustain the energy of the Holy Spirit and the Tao. Let them begin their sacred quest for the Holy Grail and Buddha's begging bowl that they might perfect the crystal chalice of the soul. And may they always be filled with the divine ambrosia of Prajnaparamita's love.

Devotees of the Mother define selfhood by upholding the truth of immaculate reality, which is the blueprint of the soul's identity in the fiery core of being. And they unravel the unreal self by discerning and extracting the threads of karma and the mind-set that created them. Then they weave in filaments of wisdom and compassion that the tapestry of being might be made whole.

So untangle your warlike elements in all their blatant and subtle manifestations—anger, resentment, sense of injustice, hatred and fanaticism. If you have a bad temper, for example, do not deny it before God, before yourself or before your peers. But have the courage to confess your fault.

Be humble and patient, and ask companions on the path to keep the flame for you, to pray for you and to uphold your body and soul through the temptations of the night.

Beseech the bodhisattvas and guardian angels for reinforcement, for they are always willing to help you. The hosts of heaven and earth will serve the soul who acknowledges the absence of the Divine Whole and asks for intercession and healing. Blessed are they who know they are poor in spirit, for they will be filled with the Holy Spirit and attain the kingdom of heaven.

What will be your affirmation of truth? What will be your refutation of error? Claim the calm Buddhic mindfulness of your Buddha-nature and your ultimate self. And as you internalize this discerning wisdom, let truth reveal to you the reality and unreality of any given situation or point of consciousness.

But do not revolve or engage in unreality, for you risk reversing the roles of the Buddha and Mara, the real self and the destructive self. For to give power to unreality is to imprison the lightning of God's splendor.

Command the atoms and molecules comprising the lesser self into the flame of living truth as you pray unto the Lord:

O God, I believe in you and in the Buddha-nature within. Help thou mine unbelief. O God, the I AM THAT I AM in me can balance my temper and my temperament and make me whole. Help thou mine imperfections. This is my earnest confession before the Christ and the Buddha, who stand at the sacred altar in the temple of my heart.

Thus you invoke the purging fires of the Buddhic light and you make progress, though sometimes painful, on the path of truth. And by abiding in truth, you are fulfilled in its integrity.

Watch out! I say. Watch out for the self-deceived ego that bombards you with its unreality, for it wants you to believe its illusions are coming from God.

Many among the human race have such a momentum of self-deception that it has become an entrenched defense mechanism of the unreal self. And that self has convinced the soul that in order to survive and be successful in the world, it must lie continually. But perpetuating deception is most damaging because it denies the real self.

Therefore, keep a balanced course as the morning star scintillates in the heavens and makes the sign of the dove descending. Listen to the approbation of the Lord within your heart: "This is my beloved Son, this is my beloved Daughter in whom I am well pleased."[3]

Examine the statements that you make. Listen to your words. Remove exaggeration, imagination and vain and proud talking calculated to impress another. Beware recounting past sins in order to provoke a reaction from fellow disciples. Resolve them instead with mercy and forgiveness in the circle of understanding friends.

Beware recounting those most sacred experiences that should be held between you and the inner Guru in the hallowed silence of the all-knowing. Beware of taking the joy of spiritual freedom and desecrating it through vulgar stories and degrading humor that appeal to the base elements of the lower self.

Feed not the demons by diverting your energies into vile speech and swearing. As Christ said, "Swear not at all, neither by heaven, for it is God's throne, nor by the earth, for it is his footstool."[4] Live, then, in truth and speak the truth. Let your reason for being echo through the words of Christ, the Galilean avatar: "To this end was I born and for this cause came I into the world, that I should bear witness unto the truth."[5]

Plant the markers of your pyramid of awareness firmly in the sands of time. And define the boundaries of your reality with poise and equanimity. This is the balancing action of the threefold flame and the equilateral triangle of the Three Jewels—the Buddha, the Dharma and the Sangha.

Be free and bear witness to the truth. Understand that the statement "God is the only power that can act" is a mantra to the sacred fire that consumes the cause and core of errors.

Withdraw the sting and the poison of the viper who tries to shame you and blame you for past mistakes. And realize that with each fall or stumble lies a gold mine of lessons, growth and wisdom. It is crucial to acknowledge mistakes and learn from them. Study their patterns so you can understand the core issues, the cause behind the effect. And as you glean wisdom from your mistakes, you will be empowered and you will be able to prevent them before they build momentum in your consciousness.

So do not turn your back on the shenanigans of your human nature and say, "It is not real, it does not exist." Errors exist in the crucible of relativity in time and space and can lead your soul astray if you deny them. Challenge the part of you that is afraid to look at mistakes, and keep it at bay through persistent mindfulness. Affirm the three jewels of your pyramid of being. And through mantra and prayer, yoga and meditation, invoke the sacred fire to draw forth the divinity of your soul. This is the path of practical wisdom to reach full Buddhahood.

Man and woman created in the image of God are co-creators with life. But they have forgotten their original calling and oneness with God, and they have lost their spiritual vision. Misusing their free will, they have miscreated, and they have polluted the soul and the elements in the earth. And in their insensitivity and ignoring of truth, they have bound and confined the energy of God the Father and the energy of Mother Earth. They have imprisoned the *vajra*'s lightning and muffled the temple bell.

Thus, in the name of the I AM THAT I AM, the creative potential of a cosmos, man and woman must withdraw all misqualified energy from matrices of imperfection and patterns of error. Now they must take the key of sacred alchemy, unlock the doors and transmute the pollution in order to redeem the energy of our Father-Mother God in all creation. They must release the power of the *vajra* and sound the temple bell.

Man and woman on planet earth have endowed evil, the energy veil, with their life essence. They have proclaimed maya as real and worshiped at the feet of the human personality while failing to discern the actualities of the now.

Be willing to call a spade a spade. Out of your love of truth, have the courage to face the sordid aspects of self. For you have yet to conquer the dweller-on-the-threshold, that self-created ghost of anger and nonforgiveness who haunts you with self-loathing.

This dweller arises daily from the depths of the subconscious as "the beast that ascendeth out of the bottomless pit"[6] to sabotage your highest dreams. Once armed with truth and compassion, you will be ready to encounter that shadow self that for aeons has conspired against the truth of your being.

To prove the law of being, you must wield the sword of truth day by day to vanquish the lesser dragons of the unreal self. For then when the ultimate tests come, you will be able to stand as David before the Goliath of your own dweller-on-the-threshold. You will be as determined as Gautama when he faced the hosts of Mara and their agenda of oppression and mediocrity.

Follow the way of the Christ and the Buddha while there is yet time and space. Stand whole in the flame of living truth that is truly the foundation of your being. This is the essence of truth that becomes the sword of truth which you wield to pierce the veil of illusion and self-deception.

Now let each worded cadence, each phrase, each thought and feeling be measured against the absolute truth of being. It is like tuning a fine instrument to perfect pitch that it may harmonize throughout the realms of existence. But also self-reflect and self-assess your sour notes and sublime tones and what conditions in your consciousness gave rise to them.

Proceed from present levels of attainment to build castles in the sky, palaces of Maitreya's enlightenment and bliss.[7] Secure the bastions of identity in that castle built upon the rock of truth in the secret chamber of your heart. This is the place where you are initiated by Lord Maitreya that you might become one with God.

And when truth means more to you than life itself, then, with the soul of Sumedha, you will gladly give your life to set free the warriors of truth, your fellow bodhisattvas of the Diamond Heart.

Therefore, be willing to keep your word, to keep the bodhisattva vows you have made to God, to all sentient beings and to your own soul. Above all, consider the equation of truth whereby the comfort of the Holy Spirit becomes the truth that you impart at any given moment to anyone. This is a bodhisattva's expedient means to liberate all souls through enlightenment.

Let truth be loyalty to the cause of the Buddha, the Dharma and the Sangha. Let it be the defense of purity and the integrity of the Mother. Let truth be the protection of every earnest soul. Let it not be twisted and misconstrued to justify and rationalize the dweller mind and its deceptions.

Truth will win if you have the courage to sustain it. For with truth comes justice, and with justice the rendering of measures of karma to the left and to the right of the scales of being.

Truth is a catalyst for progress. If you would be an instrument of truth, you must be free of all momentums of deceit and self-deceit. If you would be a catalyst for change, you must purify your motives. Stand in the flame of Reality and do not fear the ultimate exposure. For those who abide in the flame of truth have nothing to hide.

Never mind, precious ones, for the law will fulfill the exposure with or without your consent. As it is written:

There is nothing covered up that will not be uncovered, nothing hidden that will not be made known. You may take it, then, that everything you have said in the dark will be heard in broad daylight, and what you have whispered behind closed doors will be shouted from the housetops.[8]

Sooner or later the great law will uncover every element that is less than truth. Therefore, leap as a joyous emerald fire to proclaim the truth, to confess all that is undesirable! And see how compassion will strengthen and transform you. See, then, how you will embrace and become one with divinity, for you have dared to be the truth.

I am in the flame of Reality witnessing unto the truth of the ages.

I am

Gautama

of Shambhala

PRAYER TO PRAJNAPARAMITA, MOTHER OF WISDOM

Om Prajnaparamita,
Thou Mother of Wisdom,
Teach thy children truth,
Teach them fearlessness
That they may embrace truth
And overcome error with the wisdom of integrity.

Om Prajnaparamita,
Thou Mother of Wisdom,
I am thy child.
Lead me to perfect wisdom
Through loving truth.
And I in turn will free all sentient life.

May we ascend in transparent wisdom,
Transcendent wisdom,
Going beyond, going beyond,
Rising above all war and strife,
Soaring above desire, desirelessness
And reaching enlightenment's peace.
Gate Gate Paragate Parasamgate Bodhi Svaha!

CHAPTER 12

The Perfection of Resolution

The pearl in the poor one's clothes is originally round and bright; if one does not know how to find it oneself, one will count others' treasures instead....

How can it compare to recognizing your own jewel, which is worth more than billions in gold? The shine of this precious pearl is most great, as it lights up all worlds in the universe....

After having recognized this jewel, who would care for ephemeral illusions anymore?

The pearl of Buddha is the same as one's own pearl.

CHANG PO-TUAN

*Devotees Striving to Enter the Nobility
of Buddhahood:*

Those who have ensnared humanity in the lies of the
unreal self have taken the energy of God, that energy which
underlies all existence and life itself, and perverted it to
create a mask. This is the mask of maya and ego.

These forces of ignorance have skillfully manipulated
souls to forget their divine origins. They have enticed them
to identify instead with the mask of glamour and super-
ficiality. And they have enshrouded the planet with a veil
of illusion that has truly become a veil of mourning.

By and by individuals have taken into their chakras
mental and emotional effluvia, contaminating the rivers
and streams of their consciousness. As more and more
souls have allowed this to happen, the planetary network of
the collective consciousness has also become polluted.

When you are off guard, you absorb these negative

vibrations and empower the mask, the energy veil called evil. And when you act out this evil in thoughts, feelings, words and deeds, you create karma. Its energy and patterns lodge in your unconscious and subconscious.

How do you conquer this karma? You engage in perpetual mindfulness. You become faithful to your desire for *bodhi*. You embrace that karma with mercy's power of transmutation. And you resolve the psychology that compelled you to engage in the energy veil in the first place and to sustain it.

If you don't pursue a path to liberation, your returning karma continues to be magnetized to the energy patterns you have created. And enmeshed again, you act it out, compounding that karma through inordinate desire and impure motives. Is this not a vicious cycle?

Understand that as long as you deny the errors of the past and disguise them with layers of the human personality, you will always be personalizing evil.

Now let us look at a problem at the other end of the spectrum. Sometimes you feel so ashamed and guilty about mistakes and karmic debts that you get lost in the fog of your emotions and mental anguish. You forget about the Buddha-nature deep within your heart. You lose perception of your innate immortality, of God becoming God within you. Yet it is real and far more powerful than the folly of your outer mind and emotions.

In the moment when the dawn of inspiration breaks

through the fog, you behold your real self as a dazzling sun. The purity of your white-fire core rises to consume the cause and core of intentional and unintentional errors, and you experience peace and resolution. Then you are free, like a soaring dove, from the condemnation and limitation of sin.

Understand, precious ones, that the sins which are common to the human race have been imposed upon sentient life by the fallen angels, the *icchantikas* who are incapable of Buddhahood.[1] They have tattooed upon the subconscious the lie that man and woman are inherently sinful.

As you approach the altar of resolution, the eighth perfection of the law, know that you must deprive the fallen angels of their booty. And what is this booty? It is your energy, which they have used to sustain themselves, having cut themselves off from their Higher Self aeons ago.

Dissociate yourself from their masks and veils, and enter into awareness of true being. Transcend relative good and evil and abide in the immaculate void. Then you can affirm with the Master of Galilee, "The devil cometh and findeth nothing in me."[2]

Look at the faces of the fallen angels, who embodiment after embodiment have personified the energy veil. What do you see? They bear the mark of nonexistence, the grayness of the unreal self. They are like whited sepulchres—beautiful on the outside but filled with dead men's bones and every kind of corruption.[3]

Mark well my words. When I enter the fire-pearl meditation[4] and become a Buddha of the ruby ray, I send forth a laser of intense love to unlock the secret rays. And I hurl sacred fire to consume the poisonous dragons, the obstacles to your Buddhahood. When that fire unquenchable comes as the baptism of the Holy Spirit, the chaff that is the seed of the *icchantikas* is burned up in an instant and is no more.

Be free from the lie that evil is any part of your true nature and the nature of your soul. Recognize the energy veil that has been superimposed over you like a shroud, smothering your soul. It has prevented the flow of the breath of the Holy Spirit—prana and eternal ch'i—which would daily cleanse, purify and renew your life.

Take the sword of truth and pierce the masks of the unreal self. Free yourself from negative energies and patterns, those self-destructive impulses of the dweller's personality with its hollow claim to reality.

Now then, let us consider the Perfection of Resolution. This is the testing of the soul in its invincible awareness of the Whole. How can you be resolute if you do not claim the rock of truth as your foundation? How can you be immovable, as the Himalayas or the Rocky Mountains, when you don't know who you are, what you are or where you are?

Be firm as you establish yourself in the law of being. Know your identity as the I AM THAT I AM. Know your identity as a devotee of the Buddha. Proclaim it! And, like

Sumedha, know that you can become a Buddha. It is your destiny.

And to those who are destined to carve in the clay of consciousness the purity of the Divine Mother, I say, become the Mother of the World, the polarity of the Buddha. And know your identity as the I AM THAT I AM in the white fire of the Mother.

To define your real self, first experience its essence. Then allow that essence to expose all that is unlike itself within you. Allow your real self to dissolve the duality of the human mind in every manifestation. Let it dissipate the anger and unforgiving momentums of the dweller. You can do this. You have free will, so you can give your Higher Self permission to transform you.

Be willing to look at your self-created obstacles. Dig them out one by one with wrathful compassion. Then refine all that is contained in the hallowed circle of being that you call "myself." This is called making progress on the path.

The path is a spiral moving to the center of the white-fire core. Many have not entered there for myriad incarnations. Being on the path is like climbing a mountain. Some may start the trek, but after a while they come to a halt. They get stuck in a narrow pass in rocky heights. So they turn back and say: "The air is too rarified. I cannot breathe the atmosphere of Spirit. The climb is too rigorous and my pack is too heavy. I will tarry in this niche of consciousness and make the trek to the summit another time."

So they give in to procrastination. Procrastination has always been the weapon of deception employed by the fallen angel. His emissaries will always tell the soul moving toward the center of being: "Another day, another year is suitable for your surrender. Don't listen to your inner sense of cycles and put yourself under undue pressure. Wouldn't you rather be more comfortable? You can remove yourself from the garden of Maitreya for a little while. He won't mind, he'll love you anyway. It really doesn't matter.

"Don't worry about the inner walk on the path of the bodhisattvas. Your path is not their path. There are many paths. You can fulfill your vow another time. You have earned and you deserve a break to leave the path awhile."

This is the line of the fallen ones. They know your psychology, and they know exactly how to trigger your insecurities and fears. They want you to accept their logic so you can rationalize taking a detour from fulfilling your destiny. They want you to be content with a surface existence.

What will you say when Mara comes to you with his lies and serpentine logic? It is like smoke seeping through the cracks in the window and underneath the door. If you inhale the stench of the Liar and the lie, you will find yourself delaying the overcoming until you are overcome by the delay. For procrastination makes you weak. It diminishes your energies, which should be dedicated and sanctified in the crucible, the Holy Grail of alchemy divine.

The messengers of old who walked the earth as living

truth did speak of the trial by fire. This is when the soul embraces the refiner's fire that transforms base elements into gold. In this divine alchemy, angels of fire scorch the human consciousness as angels of the harvest burn the stubble of the field. They set the soul free from unreality and clear the soil for a new sowing. And in that moment of stripping, the soul experiences Buddhic illumination.

This silent flash of the lightning of the mind of God is like satori, Zen realization. This glimpse of beingness, I AM THAT I AM, is the instrument of God's grace for bodhisattvas who want to be victorious in the way of the tempter.

For in the moment of victory, you must sustain intense soul fire. And you must be constant in sustaining the fire of illumination so it will not be weakened and dispersed. For once the fire is dispersed, you cannot summon the full measure of strength required to overcome Mara and his tempters. And you must start over again to garner and concentrate wisdom's energies in order to win ultimate liberation.

Cycles of life flow according to the law of yin and yang. The yang phase is the concentration of power from the heart of God the Father. The yin phase begins when that power is released throughout the universe by God the Mother. Victory begins in the concentrated white-fire core of the divine masculine. Then comes the ritual of sustainment through the divine feminine. And triumphant joy spans the cosmos as the burst of life from the heart of our Father-Mother God.

The fallen angels understand these cycles, and they know how to pervert them and then cloak them so you will get caught in a false path. Beware of their logic and misinterpretations. For they will taunt you and try to take from you, surely as I am the Buddha of the world, your firm resolve to be unshaken by the boisterous winds that test the moorings of your tree of life.

Are your roots deep enough and firm enough to hold the trunk and branches in their place? Are you grounded in the law, O my soul, Sumedha, soul of humanity? Are your feet firmly planted in the soil of the Mother?

Take care, O my soul, to be resolute in the precepts pure. Take care when the magnetism of the lower nature draws you to dark pools of the unconscious, the underlying links to the consciousness of the fallen ones.

Make your resolution to win your victory now! No other time or space exists except the here and now. Past, present and future are contained within the now. The now is the moment of causation. The now is the moment of self-realization. And the here is the point of the precipitation of Buddhic awareness.

You cannot act in the past and you cannot act in the future. You can only act in the now to correct the wrongs of the past and to plow a straight furrow for future beginnings.

Do you see, then, how Mara, that fallen one, has stolen from the Mother and her children pearls of opportunity for self-transformation? Again and again he has pilfered segments of time and space that belonged to the Mother. He took advantage of souls caught in samsara and destroyed them.

Now, chelas of the law, seize from the fallen ones their domination of time and space. Challenge the cycles of the energy veil that they have imposed over the coordinates of time and space. For they have spun a spider's web to entangle souls of light. Take the sword of truth and of resolution strong and sweep it through that spider's web. See revealed instead starry bodies adorning the firmament of God.

Now, my soul, realize that these are the starry bodies of the saints of East and West. For they have perceived the secret rays and seized the coordinates of time and space to glorify the Mother. These are the starry crystal fragments of the Christos taking their place in the mystical body of the Buddha and the Mother. This is the mandala divine.

Wherever you are, you can become a starry body. But you must forsake the procrastinator who defies the Great Initiator, Maitreya. Do not turn your back on the flame and and walk away from the testing of your soul. Affirm your resolution. Be willing to give of yourself. Impart the elixir of life to devotees who follow you on the path of initiation under Maitreya.

You are not jellyfish! You are not protoplasm suspended in the brine! You have a starry blueprint and a skeletal framework that the Lord God has framed and draped with sacred essence of the body of the Mother.

Be swift, my soul! Be swift to invite initiation, to take it from the heart, the head and the hand of the Mother. And know that the Buddhas will release to you confirmation of being through each step of initiation. Receive these signs of victory on the path.

I am the resolution of the law within you. I am the confirmation of true being. I stand immovable upon the rock. Stand with me and we shall see the stillness of the stars after the hurricane has passed.

I am at Shambhala the Buddha of the lighthouse.

Gautama

PRAYER:
I Am Thy Holy Grail

Om Gautama Buddha   Om Maitreya Buddha
Om Jesus Christ

By divine will
May thy love and wisdom
Suffuse my soul and consciousness
That I may go forth
Into the recesses of my mind and being
To dissolve the enemy within
And become thy crystal vessel.

I am thy Holy Grail.
I am thy Buddha's bowl.
I am focalizing the white light within our planet.
I am visualizing golden illumination for all,
Weaving colors, vibrations, virtues,
Leading all sentient beings
To their divine oneness in the Trikaya.

This is my vow
And my offering
That others may live
And find hope
Of liberation through sweet enlightenment.

Prepare me, O precious ones,
That I may be thy vessel
And become all thou art.
Om Jesus Christ
Om Maitreya Buddha   Om Gautama Buddha

WHITE LOTUS MEDITATION
TO EMPOWER THE BODHISATTVA

In India the lotus is revered as a symbol of spiritual purity. It also symbolizes the soul that rises from the swamps of samsara to unfold its petals of enlightenment.

As you begin this meditation, sit comfortably and become aware of your breath. Focus within the twelve petals of your heart chakra and feel the rhythm of your heartbeat.

Meditate on the love of our Father-Mother God. As you inhale, think within your being, "I and my Father are one." When you exhale, think, "I and my Mother are one."

Visualize a lotus bud unfolding deep within your heart. See the lotus open gently, lovingly, peacefully, its petals shafts of white light.

As you envision the white-flame lotus around your heart, it consumes the obstacles to your becoming the heart, head and hand of God. Contemplate what Jesus meant when he said, "Blessed are the pure in heart, for they shall see God."

As you feel the healing purity of the lotus, you become aware that there is also a lotus of the mind and a lotus of the hand.

Now focus on the blazing lotus of your

mind. Its light dissipates negative thoughts and any sense of limitation and unworthiness. Your soul rejoices as you observe the purification of your mind.

Now place your hands on your knees, palms up, and visualize a beautiful white lotus blooming from the cup of each palm. Every time you reach out your hands to help others, see the flaming white lotus pulsating in each of your palms. And know that you have consecrated your hands to God to serve all sentient life.

Return to the twelve petals of the lotus in your heart. Visualize a white thread rising from your heart, connecting with your mind. Then see the white thread in your mind extending itself to the lotuses of your hands.

Accept this blessing, this suffusion of purity's flame, and impart it to all life. This is the empowerment from your Higher Self coursing through your chakras. It is your power to heal, to resurrect and to perfect by the laying on of hands.

ᔐ

CHAPTER 13

The Perfection of Goodwill

I dedicate whatever merit I have gained
From prostrating, making offerings,
Confessing my negativities,
Rejoicing in the virtue of others,
Requesting the Buddhas to turn the wheel of Dharma,
Requesting them to live long,
So that I may attain enlightenment
For the sake of all beings.

TIBETAN PRAYER

Bodhisattvas Seeking and Finding the Ninth Perfection of the Law:

Now hear the word of the Buddha of the flame
That speaks from within your heart.
Behold the rising spirals three,
Patterned course of solar destiny.
Behold the intertwining of Brahma, Vishnu, Shiva.
Behold the braid of sacred fire
That crowns the head of the Mother of the World.

In the ninth perfection of the law,
Discover now the sacred formula
Of the Master Alchemist,
The mystery of the three-times-three.
Goodwill is the ninth perfection,
The three-times-three.

Three-times-three is the goodwill
That integrates Creator and creation in the Whole.

Currents of blue-fire energy
Coalesce to build the pyramid of your soul.
Three-times-three is blue-fire energy
To fulfill the blueprint of God's will, goodwill.
It transforms your resolution
Into constant mindfulness of the precepts pure.

And crystal waters of the Mother cleanse
All the skandhas[1] *and soul senses*
And the four lower bodies of each one.
The power, wisdom and love of the three-times-three
In goodwill comes full circle,
Flawless blue-white diamond
Hidden in the earth of the Mother.

Let goodwill flow through the right hand and through the left, to friend and foe alike. Be like the sun that shines upon the just and the unjust. Only then can you free your own soul. Become a solar disc, a fiery crystal of Vairochana, for he is a manifestation of the Central Sun.[2] Reflect the lightning of the mind of God. Be alive and brilliant in the oneness of the three-times-three.

Dare to stand in the presence of the one who ensouls goodwill as the law of cosmos. Dare to make your aura the aura of that Radiating One, Vairochana. Stand, O my soul, in the place where the sun of goodwill caresses the mind, refreshes the body and plants a kiss, a diamond dewdrop, on the petal of the rose of the heart.

The power of the three-times-three is activated when Father-Mother energies blend harmoniously. Observe this in the interlaced triangles of the Star of David, where the ascending triangle of Mother Earth intersects the descending triangle of Father Spirit. Meditate on this symbol. The key to this mystery is the law of symmetry and the converging of spirit into matter and matter into spirit.

Contemplate the scales of Libra, the balance of the flow of energy in time and space. Contemplate the cascading and accumulating sands in each turn of the hourglass. Visualize these currents of energy through the figure eight and the double *vajra*. Meditate on the inbreath and the outbreath, on receiving and giving the solar fires and solar breath.

Behold the enlightenment of the law.
Tend the fires of goodwill
For self-proclaimed enemies,
For the idolators of your person,
For those who come at eventide
To bask in the fires of your hearth,
To sup at your table
And to hear the word of wisdom.
Observe the flow,
Then become the flow of Tao.
And see how goodwill is the key
To the redemption of all energy
Imprisoned in the dungeon of former selves
That you have created by free will.

Now will another self.
Create it in the image of God.
Decipher the code of alchemy
As you discover the molecules of goodwill
Flowing through all form and substance,
Through the air and through the water,
In the earth and in the fire.
These translucent spheres, like sparkling prana,
Are thoughtforms I release
From the mind of the Lord of the World.
Perceive energy moving throughout a cosmos
And the solar systems of the atoms.
Observe the power of goodwill
And learn now this perfection to instill
In every chakra, in every point of flow.

For as above, so below,
The lightning of the mind of God,
The diamond vajra,
Now flashes through each soul dedicated to goodwill.
Boundless energy!
Boundless creativity!
Freedom to move and to be in love
The perfection that you are
Is unlocked by the key of goodwill.

Let love be a burning fire in your heart. Let it transmute
the hatred of the aggressor, of the professor who professes

anti-God and the philosophy of the Liar and the lie. Let charity be the handmaid of goodwill. Let it be the ruby ray that pierces, like a laser beam, the malintent of those who plot the death of Christ and Buddha and the anointed one, who is your real self. Let charity be a flame that consumes the vengeance of the fallen ones, for they are jealous of the Mother and her children and their hallowed circle of oneness. They denied the Mother long ago through nonforgiveness and anger's fear.

Let goodwill expand now. Let it expand as a fiery blue sphere growing, growing in the hearts of devotees of the Buddha and the Mother.

I walk the earth strewing flowers along the pathways, in the valleys and the mountains, anticipating the coming of the Mother. And I search for devotees glowing in the meditation of the blue sphere of goodwill, glowing in the action of goodwill. I look for eyes that sparkle, for hearts abounding in joy and love. I look for smiling, upturned faces waiting on the eternal sun. I seek those who will listen to the word of goodwill and then run to do that will, to become that word, to prove the law as love in action in serving all sentient life.

> *Keep on keeping on,*
> *Lovers of the Buddha,*
> *Children of the Mother.*
> *Be dispensers of goodwill*
> *And mark the place where God does will*

The fullness of himself
In form and formlessness,
In the sanctuary of being,
In the soul and in the mind,
In the threefold fire
Burning on the altar of the heart.
Be goodwill
And see how God will fulfill himself
In the diamond in the center of the flame.

Now this day let that flame
Consume all desire for vengeance.
Let your desiring be instead
For the liberation of each soul.
Study the Dharma,
Meditate upon the Dharma,
And impart the Dharma to a cosmos.
Then watch intently
As atoms of goodwill,
The components of God's being,
Express the geometry of goodwill
As a mandala spanning time and space.
Keep the image of perfection
As a diamond without flaw.

In the heart of the flame,
I am the Buddha of goodwill.

Gautama

PRAYER TO COMFORT
ALL SENTIENT LIFE

O Buddha of my heart!
O Buddha of my soul!
Trikaya of true being!
I would gladly give my all
If with Lord Gautama
I could be the Dharmakaya
The Sambhogakaya and the Nirmanakaya
And permeate the universes with healing
*   illumination.*

I would remain on earth a pilgrim of peace.
I would remain in heaven in the peace
*   of the Divine Whole.*
I would remain as a comforter to all sentient life,
Helping beings in all realms and evolutions—
A Good Samaritan to the wounded
*   and the suffering,*
A friend to the friendless,
The voice of conscience to the conscienceless,
Father to the fatherless,
Mother to the motherless,
Brother and sister to the orphan,

Giving even my body and my blood
To those who hunger and thirst after
   righteousness.

I would heal the sick, cleanse the lepers,
   raise the dead
And cast out the hosts of Mara in
   Gautama Buddha's name;
For freely I have received and freely I will give.

I would be an eternal light,
Like Dipamkara and the Buddhas past,
   present and future,
To dispel the darkness of a suffering world.
May the lightning of my coming Buddhahood
Penetrate time and space.
This is my prayer and my meditation
   in this hour.

~

CHAPTER 14

The Perfection of Indifference

In the midst of the mountains
There are many fellow Buddhists
Chanting sutras and meditating together
For the sake of all life.
From the city walls, people gazing toward the peaks
Only observe white clouds.

WANG WEI

Bodhisattvas Fulfilling the Ten Perfections:

Approach the tenth perfection of the law with reverence, the reverence you feel when beholding the Himalayas or the Rocky Mountains. It is the delight you find in the wildflowers of a rolling meadow, the wonder you sense when you come upon a tumbling stream that dances in the light of a spring morning. The stream is like the Mother anticipating the coming of the Buddha. You sit on its banks, lined with yellow-green willows, and gaze at the rolling meadows as you begin to meditate.

I am the Buddha, and I am with you as you meditate on the stream of Tao, where the meadow of the Mother reaches the boundaries of the Spirit. Enter these waters and mark the levels of consciousness where I am. Explore the depths of my origins in the fiery glacier, the crystal snows and the summit of the primordial Dhyani Buddha, Vajrasattva.

I am the source of the river of life, abiding in the

mountain of the I AM THAT I AM. From exalted heights rushing waters descend to greet the meadow of the Mother. And from the mountains to the valleys, I am the soul pursuing essence. I shall be transformed, as water becomes air and air becomes fire. By this alchemy the soul cradled in the earth is born again in the crucible of fire.

Now perceive the power of the three-times-three, the foundation of the Trinity, awaiting the tenth perfection of the law. Multiply the first three perfections by the second three. Then take that total and multiply it again by the final three, and see the light bursting through the mastery of the tenth.

Let the perfections of alms, precepts and renunciation merge into one balanced triangle of power, wisdom and love. They are one flame, brilliant white, like the shield and sword of Spirit glistening in the sun. Let the perfections of wisdom, courage and patience become a single taper to light the candle on the altar of the Buddha. Let the perfections of truth, resolution and goodwill become the foundation to build the temple of the Mother.

Now 1 times 2 is 2, and 2 times 3 is 6. Six, then, is the number of the first three perfections of the law. And 4 times 5 is 20, and 20 times 6 is 120. Thus two 6s plus 0 reveal the number of the second three perfections of the law to be 120.

Follow my numbers carefully and be mindful of the base of nine as I show you the key to the mystery of the three-times-three. Seven times 8 is 56, and 56 times 9 is 504. Thus 504 is the number of the ultimate three.

Now let us add the digits of our pyramid of the perfections: 6 plus 1 plus 2 plus 0 equals 9. Nine plus the power of the ten (symbolized in the zero) is the sign of the first and the second three perfections. Five plus 0 plus 4 equals 9 in the power of the ten in the final three perfections of the law.

Six times 120 equals 720. And 7 plus 2 plus 0 equals 9 in the power of the ten as the multiplication factor of the first two sets of three perfections. Now multiply 720 times 504 and see the power of the three-times-three—362,880. Once again add the digits—3 plus 6 plus 2 plus 8 plus 8 plus 0 gives 27 in the power of the ten. When you again add this sum, 2 plus 7 plus 0 equals 9 in the power of the ten. Nine is the magic number. Resolve to perfect these perfections of the law by the power of the ten.

Contemplate the components of the numeral 9 and its transformation into 10. Behold the circle of the Mother raised to the top of the vertical line of the Father. This signifies the raising of the Mother light from the base chakra to the crown through the spinal altar. This is the sacrifice of one's attainment of the three-times-three. It is the ascent into heaven to bring back to the altar of the earth a mark, an understanding of the next step on the bodhisattva path, so that others may follow. Thus we have the perfections ten to transform conquerors in the earth into Buddhas in a world to be.

What, then, is the tenth perfection of the law? It is the blessing of the three-times-three and the nine-times-nine. I call it indifference. The one who masters the nine perfections is not exalted by human praise nor condemned by human blame but calmly receives hot and cold, sweet and foul. This equanimity arises from constant mindfulness and fulfilling the mathematics of the soul.

By the alchemy of the three-times-three, the Mother purifies the vices and the virtues of her children. She embodies the grace of the three-times-three, the grace of Shambhala and the threefold flame.

The tenth perfection is the balance of desire and desirelessness. It is the point where the active and the passive merge. And through it the power of the three-times-three is multiplied by tens, by hundreds, by thousands, by millions, by billions and beyond.

The Perfection of Indifference is your sustained intensity that determines how much energy can be entrusted to your care. The three-times-three becomes the 9, the 90, the 900, the 9,000, the 9 million or the 9 billion according to your attainment of indifference.

Transcend the ego and be unattached to mockery or praise, pleasure or pain, poverty or riches, adulation or indignation. This is the tenth perfection of the law—indifference to the gratitude or ingratitude of mortals, indifference to their cursings or the garlands of their approbation.

Do not be moved from your point of centeredness as you pursue and subdue the ego. For the ego is the impostor of your true nature in Buddha and Christ, in the Mother and the Holy Spirit. Now let the Ten Perfections of the Law be the pillars of fire that expose and consume the ego and the unreal self.

Be the world conqueror! Take the sword of the sacred Word and, with supreme indifference, invoke the secret rays to dissolve your dweller-on-the-threshold.

Cultivate and practice the Ten Perfections of the Law. Be diligent and you will gain the momentum of the nine-times-nine. Be tenacious and undaunted like the ox herder who tamed the ox. For in so doing, he disciplined his own nature and overcame mortality, sensuality and rode the bull home.

Coming Home on the Ox's Back
One of ten paintings illustrating
the stages of Zen discipline
by Shubun, a fifteenth-century
Japanese Zen priest.

Enter now the champion of the flame.
Enter now the one who fears not,
Who has nothing to claim as his own
Or to lose except to choose
The victory of the Buddha and the Mother.

See how the victor bold meets every cunning
Of the cowardice of the Taurus creation,
Defending the light of the Buddha's station.
See how the ox herder watches every move,
To master emotion
And discern vibration,
To prove he is not discouraged
But with noble art he disciplines the enemy within.

Caught off guard,
The bull snorts and trots away
To elude the Buddhic one,
The Buddha of the sun.
But the mantle of the Lord of the World
Empowers the humble ox herder
To use his tether, harness and whip
To subdue the bull's unyielding nature.

Seeing the Ox   **Catching the Ox**

See how he wields them deftly–
A prophet in his own right,
Like Elisha, who smote the waters
By Elijah's might.

The bull resists,
Blinded by the passions
Of his two-eyed vision.
But with all the borrowed energy
Vested in his animality,
He cannot win against the soul
Who has mastered the ten,
The Ten Perfections of the Law.

Now content to be led by the nose,
The bull follows the ox herder's lead
And enters the path of gentleness,
His Buddha-nature now freed.

And, lo, the champion,
The master over all sensation
And the bull creation,
Stands in the center alone
And transcends the self and not-self,
In the circle of the One.[1]
He is the victor!
He is ready for his incarnation
As the Buddha in the world to be.

I am Gautama in the center of the flame, the great source of your soul and mine. I am the Tathagata, the thirteenth Buddha of the fourteen Shining Ones.[2]

I have released to you the second tier of my teaching on the Buddha and the Mother. For the twelve disciples in the mandala of the Lord of All the World have pursued and won the Ten Perfections of the Law. So our promise is fulfilled.[3]

I am the Buddha. I come quietly. I have come to show you the way that you might return to the flame as the Tathagata, the Thus-Come One.

Summon now your divinity.

Gautama

PRAYER:
Lead Me to Shambhala

Om Buddha
Om Mother
O Divine Mother,
In thy power and sweet love
And in the presence of all the Buddhas
You have given birth to,
I call to you:
Lead me to Shambhala—
City of light, city of the sun, city of the soul.
Lead me to Shambhala,
Star of the East within the Eden of my sacred self.
Smiling upon me,
Kindred Buddhas and bodhisattvas of that
    holy city
Greet me with a holy kiss.
I am enraptured in bliss
As I vow to share this joy and wisdom
With all sentient life.
I abide this day in Shambhala,
City of my God.
Pilgrim of peace from earth,

I pray to the Five Dhyani Buddhas,
To the Buddhas of the Ten Directions
And to the Buddhas past, present and future:
May my soul become one with thee.
As I dwell in this city of the Eternal Day,
Tears of joy mingle with tears of the bodhisattvas
In love's resolution.
Into this starry city
Through the gateway of the secret love star
I see my Buddhahood before me.
I am come,
The Tathagata,
Merging my all with the One,
The immaculate void.
O star of my Buddhic essence,
I AM THAT I AM.
Om

~

MEDITATION:
Your Pilgrimage to Shambhala

To enter Shambhala is to enter a chamber in the mind of God. Through practicing meditation and visualization on the bodhisattva path, you can realize the kingdom within and the kingdom without.

On your pilgrimage to this City of the Sun, you come to a bridge of glistening marble. You can already see Shambhala on the horizon. It is a white island of sandy beaches suspended in a sapphire sea.

You walk along the bridge, your thoughts awash in the rhythm of the waves and your heart suffused in the rays of the eternal sun. All else fades as you breathe in the fire breath of God and contemplate your love for him and your bodhisattva vows.

As you reach the end of the marble bridge, you open a gate just as a flock of doves swirls up into the air. Watching them disappear, you notice the golden dome of the main temple rising above the summit of the island.

You follow a footpath that winds through exquisite gardens, rock formations and waterfalls. Occasionally you pass a grotto where Buddhas meditate, sending forth shimmering light.

Reaching another level, you are delighted by terraces with flame-fountains of various hues. Banners representing the virtues of Buddhas and cosmic beings surround a series of alabaster temples. A throng of bluebirds soars by, beckoning you on to the golden-domed temple. The temple is at the top of a high pyramid with a wide white marble staircase.

You walk up the marble steps and enter the temple. At the door you see vases filled with your favorite flowers. You have entered a shrine of love, sweet love.

Kuan Yin, the Bodhisattva of Mercy, greets you with an embrace and a transfer of mercy's flame from her heart. She gives you an elixir of wisdom and compassion to drink. Its rich, deep violet color is flecked with gold.

As you enter the main hall under the golden dome, you perceive the starry bodies of billions of bodhisattvas gathering into spherical formation around Gautama Buddha. The Lord of the World is seated on a sapphire-blue lotus throne. You join them in meditation.

Over the central altar you observe a star growing brighter and brighter until the Buddha Dipamkara and his divine consort emerge out of its light. They are clothed in mother-of-pearl robes and wear hats reminiscent of those worn by Tibetan lamas. Dipamkara leads a holy mantra in an unknown tongue as flames of blue, gold and pink appear in front of him.

You walk up to Dipamkara and he blesses you on your forehead. Then you take a piece of sandalwood and light it from the blue, pink and gold flames. Holding the threefold light close to your heart, you return to your meditation seat.

The billions of bodhisattvas around you also hold flames. Your three-dimensional mandala begins to expand, being filled out by billions of Buddhas and their retinues.

Soon the entire planet is ensphered in your mandala of Buddhas and bodhisattvas. You extend your light to the inhabitants of earth, strengthening and inspiring all sentient life. Now the earth is enfolded in whirling blue, gold and pink flames that begin to change to mother-of-pearl light.

You realize that all sentient life has attained enlightenment and the earth has become a star, freedom's star.

⌣

Notes

CHAPTER 1

1. Mystics throughout the ages have pursued spiritual liberation through purifying and then raising their feminine and masculine energies from the base-of-the-spine chakra to the crown. In India this is described as the yogic weaving of the *ida* and *pingala* energies up the *sushumna* in the spine. This divine dance of feminine and masculine (yin and yang) is represented through many symbols, such as the T'ai Chi in Chinese Taoism. In the West it has been symbolized in the caduceus, a staff of two intertwined snakes topped by a pair of wings. The Greek god Hermes is shown holding this staff, and physicians have adopted it as their symbol.

2. Imagine being surrounded by a vast arc of cascading waters over two miles wide. That's the width of four Niagara Falls. These 275 waterfalls known as Iguaçu plummet hundreds of feet, driving expansive mists into the air. Some of the falls deflect off rocky ledges, creating myriad rainbows that play upon the rising mists.

   Iguaçu, which comes from Guarani for "great water," also refers to the Iguaçu River, which plunges into the falls on the border of Brazil and Argentina before joining the Paraná River at the nexus where Brazil, Argentina and Paraguay meet.

   In the esoteric tradition *Iguaçu* means "I am! I was! I shall be!" "I was" symbolizes the water before it reaches the break. It's the past. "I am" signifies the water when it breaks into the falls. It's the now, representing the descent and release of energy from God into the heart chakra of the devotee and the planet. The future, the "I shall be," is depicted in the waters flowing out from the bottom of the falls. The mists represent the crystal fire mist—the spiritual energy of precipitation, transmutation, creation and innovation through union with God's consciousness.

   Visualizing Iguaçu Falls can become a meditation on the victory for one's soul and all sentient life in the eternal now.

CHAPTER 2

1. The utopic Shangri-la in James Hilton's novel *Lost Horizon,* also made into a movie, has inspired many a heart and imagination. Perhaps Shangri-la

stirred a soul memory of Shambhala, a legendary Buddhist kingdom believed to be in Central Asia.

Tibetan and Mongolian people have been fascinated with Shambhala for several hundred years. They believe it's somewhere north of Tibet and that a lineage of enlightened kings has ruled and guarded its secret teachings for centuries. They also believe that Shambhala is the sacred source of the teachings of Kalachakra, an advanced meditation system introduced in Tibet in the eleventh century.

Tibetan Buddhists associate this sacred kingdom with the Future Buddha Maitreya, whom they believe will emerge as a saviour to establish a golden age when the world has nearly succumbed to chaos and decay.

His Holiness the Dalai Lama, the exiled ruler of Tibet, feels that the kingdom has a material existence in this world, but one must be highly developed spiritually to find or recognize it. Not even His Holiness can say where Shambhala is located.

Shambhala is Sanskrit for "source of happiness." Esoterists call Shambhala the "White Island" and believe it was located in the Gobi Sea, now the Gobi Desert, which spans areas of Mongolia and China. Geologists confirm that the area of the Gobi Desert had indeed been covered by water at one time.

According to esoteric versions of the legend, a dark age descended on earth thousands of years ago, causing the ancient Buddha Dipamkara ("Kindler of Lights") to respond with great compassion. He and a retinue of bodhisattvas came from another dimension to help humanity reconnect with their divine spark of Buddha-nature.

On the island they built several white temples, with domes and spires, along with terraces, gardens, flame-fountains and pools. Dipamkara, also known as Sanat Kumara, established a spiritual focus of love, wisdom and power in the main temple and extended a thread of light to the heart of everyone on earth.

But as time passed, the residents of Shambhala began to forget their spiritual identity and rejected their divine heritage and mission. Some of them called themselves "Realists." Eventually they constituted about half of Shambhala's population. At this low point, one day when Dipamkara and his consort were performing a sacred ceremony in the main temple, the Realists barged in and began mocking them. Suddenly there was a rumbling sound and Shambhala was instantly withdrawn into the etheric realms. All that was left were the Realists standing in the middle of a desert.

Although Shambhala is no longer physical, its subtle influences still radiate throughout the planet. For a visual description of ancient Shambhala, see meditation on pages 158-60.

CHAPTER 3

1. The fourteen stations of the cross represent the fourteen key events and spiritual initiations in Jesus' life from the time he was condemned to death to his crucifixion and burial in the sepulchre. For example, at the second station Jesus bore the cross on the way to Calvary. This was his initiation to carry the weight of world karma and give humanity a reprieve from karmic consequences so that they might develop themselves spiritually. This was part of the bodhisattva path of Jesus Christ.

2. Buddhas and highly evolved bodhisattvas have attained six supernatural powers to liberate themselves and all sentient beings. Some of these powers are similar to those Jesus demonstrated in his miracles, such as being able to walk on water and read the hearts and minds of others.

The first five powers include the ability to hear divine voices, to penetrate minds, to see into the future, to fly, to become invisible, to remember past lives of oneself and others, and to know the birth and death of all beings. The sixth power is the ability to extinguish one's impurities and passions in order to liberate the soul.

3. The Queen Mother of the West has been revered in China for at least three thousand years. Countless devotees, from peasants to the ruling elite, have worshiped her in her various roles as they were revealed throughout the centuries. She was known as a deity for the western direction and as a goddess who commanded the constellations and brought rain and successful harvests. She was believed to be the ancestress of the Chinese people, a member of a council of deities overseeing the destiny of humanity, and the instructor of legendary and historical rulers as well as the embodiment of the supreme feminine (yin), the bestower of immortality, and the role model and protector of Taoist priestesses and adepts.

Devotees yearned to be with her in her spiritual retreat, believed to be in the Kunlun Mountains in northwest China. They anticipated experiencing bliss and eternal youth in her retreat as they mingled with fantastic creatures, sage-spirits and the Queen Mother's sons and daughters, who were immortals. They could stroll through her vast gardens of magical plants, enjoy her enchanted brook and turquoise pool, marvel at her fountain made of gems and partake of her peaches of immortality. The mountain where her retreat was located was considered the *axis mundi,* the link between heaven and earth, and so beyond the influence of the physical sun that it was illuminated by a creature known as the Torch Dragon.

Also known as the Golden Mother, the Queen Mother of the West is depicted wearing a crown that originally may have been a crown of stars. Later her crown resembled a loom device, symbolizing her role as weaver and maintainer of the fabric of the universe.

She is usually accompanied by three green birds who bring her food and sometimes by a tiger and a dragon who protect her. In her role as the Keeper of the Peaches of Immortality, she is attended by a phoenix, who represents eternal life.

One White Lotus Buddhist sect that emerged in the sixteenth century believed that the Queen Mother of the West and Kuan Yin were incarnations of their chief deity, the Eternal Mother. ("White Lotus" refers to a number of Buddhist sects in China associated with the Future Buddha Maitreya.)

The Eternal Mother was believed to have existed before the creation of the cosmos. She gave birth to yin and yang and to the original ancestors of humankind. They in turn gave birth to 960,000,000 sons and daughters and countless auspicious stars. These sons and daughters of the Eternal Mother were Buddhas and immortals. When she sent them to the "red dust" world of samsara, their heads were encircled with light and they wore garments of five colors. They also bore the Three Jewels of Buddhism.

But eventually they forgot who they were as they pursued fame, money and sensuality. So the Eternal Mother grieved and began to send messengers to remind them of their divine identity and that it was time to return home to her womb, nirvana. The Eternal Mother's messengers included Buddhas like Dipamkara, Gautama and the Future Buddha Maitreya.

4.   After Gautama passed into his final nirvana, his alms bowl became one of the most venerated relics of the Buddhist world. The bowl is said to have supernatural powers and is thought to be the inspiration for the Western legend of the Holy Grail.

Four deva-rajas (celestial kings) presented Gautama with the sacred bowl after he gained enlightenment. At first they gave him four alms bowls made of gold. Gautama, however, refused them, feeling it was inappropriate to receive such valuable gifts. But the deva-rajas did not give up. They offered him a succession of bowls made of silver, crystal, lapis lazuli, pearl and other precious stones, but still he would not accept them. Finally, each of the deva-rajas presented Gautama with a dark violet stone bowl. Gautama received the four bowls, put them together and compressed them into one.

5.   John 6:53.

CHAPTER 4

1.   Tathagata, or 'Thus-Come One,' is one of the highest titles of a Buddha. Gautama used this title to refer to himself and other Buddhas. The Tathagata is the one who comes to do what other Buddhas have done—engage and master the absolute way of cause and effect and attain perfect wisdom.

2.   Nature spirits of every form and manifestation are crucial to our spiritual and physical progress. Also called elementals, they help create and sustain our earth so that we may have a platform for our souls to evolve and gain enlightenment. The four types of elementals are gnomes, sylphs, salamanders and undines, and they sustain the elements of earth, air, fire and water. In a hierarchy of different levels and types of beings, they serve under the direction of the Elohim and the angel devas. As we get to know them and work with them as precious friends, they help us prepare our four lower bodies and our soul to receive the light of illumination.

Elementals need our support in prayers and mantras in this day and age when the pollution of the human race has become a great burden to them. Intoning the Om for harmony is one way to help them.

The elementals have been the students of the Buddha for ages and they are in complete rapport with his soul. You see how Gautama as a little boy was inspired by the digging into the earth element and he experienced bliss. This memory later inspired him to pursue meditation to become a Buddha.

When Gautama was challenged by Mara during his meditation, he responded by touching the earth. This was his gesture to beseech the elementals, the angel devas, *gandharvas* and other beings of light to bear witness to his right to sit under the Bodhi tree and win enlightenment. As he touched the ground, his light penetrated the earth. For the light of the Buddha penetrates the earth through elemental life as they conquer the hordes of Mara and hold the balance until all sentient life is able to receive the Three Jewels of the Buddha, the Dharma and the Sangha.

3.   *Gandharvas* are fairylike celestial musicians who sing the glories of divinity. They are the devas of divine music and their song resounds throughout the world in subtle essence. "There is the deep [bellow] of the sea, the sighing of the wind in the trees, the roar of the mountain torrent, the music of stream, river

and waterfall, which together with many others form the mighty song of Nature. . . . This is but the echo in the physical world of a far grander sound, that of the Being of the *[gandharvas]*," explains author of esotericism C. W. Leadbeater.

4. That Gautama Buddha gained enlightenment under the Bodhi tree is another testament to his friendship with the elementals. The Bodhi tree was a fig tree (Ficus religiosa), popularly known as a pipal. This tree of enlightenment became an important pilgrimage site, and cuttings of it were taken as far as Sri Lanka.

CHAPTER 5

1. The Mother of the World, like the Eternal Mother, is a timeless office in hierarchy of one empowered by the Father to give birth to the Buddhas. In the Agni Yoga teachings, the Mother of the World is the matriarch and initiator of the hierarchy of spiritual beings involved with this planet. She is also the spiritual mother of all the Christed Ones and Buddhas throughout history.

2. The Goddess Kundalini was originally the Hindu deification of the mother fire or supreme power in the base-of-the-spine chakra (see note 1 for chapter 1). The Goddess Kundalini is also associated with the fierce Hindu goddess Kali, the consort of Shiva.

It was an accepted practice for Buddhists in India and throughout the Far East to adopt Hindu deities into their beliefs. The sun god Surya, Indra, Shiva and the goddess of fortune and beauty, Lakshmi, are all examples of Hindu deities who were included in the Buddhist pantheon.

3. Salt, as a vital element that sustains life, has spiritual significance in Western religion and in the tradition of alchemy. In the Old Testament it symbolized loyalty, constancy and virtue. Jesus called his followers "the salt of the earth."

Paracelsus, who established a revolutionary school in medical chemistry in the sixteenth century, was an alchemist in the Hermetic tradition. He believed that the principles underlying salt, mercury and sulfur represented a trinity that was the source of all material substances. This was a concept he gleaned from Arabian alchemy. Salt represented the physical body, the tangible and the qualities of incombustibility and nonvolatility. Mercury, as spirit, symbolized fusibility and volatility. Sulfur, which stood for the soul, represented inflammability.

This trinity is also found in Chinese, Greek and Egyptian alchemy, where salt is understood as the yin quality of receiving. It is receiving energy with your left hand, taking it into your body and mind and then focusing it through divine love. This is how it is transformed through the alchemy of the whirling

T'ai Chi into the active yang. Then it will become the *action* of precipitation. Mercury represents yang energy and the understanding and power of movement of molecules as they coalesce into form.

But nothing happens with these two elements without the third element as a catalyst. Sulphur is the catalyst in this alchemy and it represents the pressure of wisdom's desire to create and precipitate. When the alchemy is complete, you can release it through the right hand as a blessing, such as we see in the mudras of the Buddhas and the Christ. So this alchemy comes full circle, and we understand why salt was sprinkled as a blessing in ancient times.

In the esoteric understanding of this trinity, the synthesis of the divine attributes of love, wisdom and power gives birth to the universal Mother, who is born out of the fiery nucleus of the threefold flame. This universal Mother is the element that is the antithesis of this thesis of the Trinity. And in turn, the union of the Trinity with the Mother becomes the accumulation of energy and its synthesis that produces numerous manifestations.

So when you engage in divine alchemy, whether it is to realize a point of illumination, a transformation or even a material substance, the key element is the Mother. This is the power of the Mother—the Queen Mother of the West, Mother Mary, the Eternal Mother, Kali, the Mother of the World or Kuan Yin, who became known in China as a feminine being.

It is significant that the Queen Mother of the West's kingdom has been associated with amazing minerals and that a vast salt bed from an ancient sea flanks one area on the north side of the Kunlun Mountains.

CHAPTER 6

1.   When you pass the initiations of the fourteen stations of the cross to attain Christhood, you have to make a decision. You can keep that attainment to yourself and walk away into the hills, never to be heard from again. Or you can offer that Christhood as a gift to help and uplift others. And in the alchemy of surrendering your attainment, God can then take it, multiply it and return it to you in greater measure. This renunciation of your Christhood is the fifteenth station of the cross. This is the bodhisattva vow to not enter nirvana till all sentient life is free.

CHAPTER 7

1.   From *Mother of the World* (New York: Agni Yoga Society, 1956), pp. 15-16, 17.

CHAPTER 8

1.   When we think about the infinite realms of Buddhas and bodhisattvas and their continual transcendence in God—truly a miracle unfolding more miracles— we may begin to doubt that we could ever manifest such light and illumination. "But the strange fact is that when a door opens and a light shines from an unknown source into the dark chamber of consciousness, all the time- and space-limitations dissolve away," explains Buddhologist D. T. Suzuki. "And we make a Simhanada (lion-roar), 'Before Abraham was, I am,' or 'I alone am the honoured one above and below all the heavens.'" See D. T. Suzuki, "Mahayana and Hinayana Buddhism, or the Bodhisattva-ideal and the Sravaka-ideal, as Distinguished in the Opening Chapter of the Gandavyuha," *Eastern Buddhist* 6(1):10–11.

2.   The secret chamber of the heart is an eight-petaled chakra often illustrated to the left side of one's heart chakra (see figure on page 108). The eight petals represent the mastery of the qualities of the seven chakras through Christic attainment and the integration of that mastery in the eighth ray. The secret chamber of the heart is the sanctuary of the Buddha and the secret rays. It is the place where the threefold flame abides, where you encounter the inner guru, and where the laws of the cosmos are inscribed as the Eightfold Path of the Buddha.

3.   *Virya* is the energy and willpower of a bodhisattva. It is the impetus and source underlying the principles that lead to enlightenment.

4.   Kuan Yin's weapons and other attributes are reflections of her compassion and wisdom as she intervenes and assists all who call to her. Forty-one of these attributes are described in the Chinese Buddhist text *Thousand Hands, Thousand Eyes, Kuan Shih Yin Bodhisattva Great Compassionate Heart Dharani (Invocation)* (Taisho 1064).

5.   Matt. 28:18.

CHAPTER 9

1.   Wisdom and compassion form the yin and yang aspects of the bodhisattva path. Buddhologist Guy Newland explains that they are "mutually influential consciousnesses. Each augments, activates, and sets the tone for the other at every stage of the path." We pursue wisdom because we have compassion for ourselves and for our loved ones. We want to be free and we want them to be free. On the other hand, as we attain greater degrees of wisdom, greater fires of mercy expand the height, breadth and depth of our hearts. So the more wisdom we have, the more we can express our compassion for others

through the solutions wisdom inspires. And the more compassion we have, the more we expand our capacity to embody wisdom.

2.   Archangel Michael is the most revered angel in Jewish, Christian and Islamic scriptures. He and his legions of angels respond to prayers for physical and spiritual protection. The Lokapalas are the guardians of the world in Buddhist tradition. Each protects the Dharma as he oversees one of the four quadrants of space.

3.   Brahma, Vishnu and Shiva form the Hindu Trinity of Creator, Preserver and Destroyer. Brahma embodies the divine desire that inspired the creation of the world. Vishnu conveys mercy and virtue to sustain the world. Shiva represents the sacred fire that destroys evil.

4.   Asanga was the founder of the Yogachara school of Buddhism in India in the fourth century A.D. Through advanced meditation he communed with Maitreya, was initiated by him and received new teachings, including the understanding of Trikaya, the three bodies of the Buddha.

CHAPTER 10

1.   Vajrasattva, whose name means "diamond being," is a meditation Buddha who presides over all the spiritual beings depicted in Tantric mandalas. He is the synthesis of the Five Dhyani Buddhas and embodies all their attainment as well as the five secret rays. Devotees who desire purification and healing invoke his intercession through his hundred-syllable mantra or a shortened form, which is Om Vajrasattva Hum.

The name Vajrasattva refers not only to a divine being but also to a state of attainment. Followers of Vajrayana Buddhism pursue the path of transcendence so they can also become a Vajrasattva diamond-being.

2.   The Golden Mantra is the mantra of Padmasambhava, who is called the Precious Guru (Guru Rinpoche) by Tibetan and other Buddhist devotees. He brought Buddhism to Tibet from India in the eighth century.

3.   See the stupa in the background of "The Three Bodies of Your Buddha-Nature" on page xxii of the introduction.

4.   Mark 4:39.

5.   The *vajra* and the ritual bell are symbols of the divine masculine and divine feminine in Tibetan Buddhism. The *vajra*, or *dorje*, conveys the meaning of the indestructible diamondlike essence of reality. As a symbol of the divine masculine, it represents the bodhisattva's *upaya*, or skillful means, to convey the teaching to all levels of beings. The bell, or *drilbu*, symbolizes the divine

feminine and the bodhisattva's wisdom to save all sentient beings. The double *vajra* and *drilbu* begin the chapters of this text.

6. I Cor. 13:4–7.

7. Kali is a manifestation of the Divine Mother and embodies the dynamic, primal energy that destroys ignorance. She releases the power of disintegration so that the soul might be liberated. Kali is the benefactor for those who strive to become one with God.

8. *The Heart of God: Prayers of Rabindranath Tagore,* ed. Herbert F. Vetter (Boston: Charles E. Tuttle Co., 1997), p. 45.

CHAPTER 11

1. There are ten qualities, or abilities, that a bodhisattva develops to realize and embody the Diamond Heart: (1) absolute intuiting and penetrating of truth, (2) the saving of all sentient beings, (3) exalting all the Buddha-worlds, (4) extending oneself in good deeds beyond the call of duty, (5) serving all Buddhas, (6) realizing the truth of the Dharma, (7) cultivating patience and endurance, (8) fulfilling one's dharma and mission with great devotion, (9) perfecting one's works and (10) helping everyone fulfill their vows and accomplish their spiritual goals.

2. Prajnaparamita is the Buddhist goddess who personifies the highest form of transcendent wisdom. Her name means "perfection of wisdom." Since the Buddhas realize their enlightenment through her transcendent wisdom, she is known as the Mother of the Buddhas.

3. Matt. 3:17; 17:5; II Pet. 1:17.

4. Matt. 5:34, 35.

5. John 18:37.

6. Rev. 11:7.

7. In the *Gandavyuha (Flower Garland) Sutra,* a little boy named Sudhana searches for enlightenment and eventually encounters Maitreya, who stands in front of a remarkable pavilion. Maitreya begins to extol Sudhana's virtues using numerous similes, such as comparing the thought of enlightenment to an alchemical elixir that turns bronze into gold.

Then Maitreya opens the pavilion, which is as high as the sky and expands throughout space, revealing beautiful palaces made of precious stones and gardens filled with trees, birds, flowers and works of art. There are numerous other magnificent pavilions as well. According to curator and art historian Jan Fontein: "There is perfect interpenetration and non-obstruction between them. All are in one, one in all, yet not interfering with each other, harmoniously interpenetrat-

ing. With Maitreya's aid Sudhana concentrates and enjoys a glimpse of enlightenment: all obstructions disappear from his thought. He finds himself in all the
pavilions simultaneously, and in each one the bodhisattva Maitreya is engaged
in good works in one or other of the worlds in the universe."

8.   Luke 12:2, 3 (New English Bible).

CHAPTER 12

1.   William Edward Soothill and Lewis Hodous, comps., *A Dictionary of
Chinese Buddhist Terms* (Delhi: Motilal Banarsidass Publishers, 1937), pp. 9b,
464b–465a, 483a; and *The Encyclopedia of Eastern Philosophy and Religion*
(Boston: Shambhala, 1994), p. 151.

2.   John 14:30.

3.   Matt. 23:27.

4.   *Fire-pearl* is the Chinese term for a ruby. The ruby ray is an intense and
holy love that is developed through the path of sacrifice, surrender, selflessness, and service to uplift all sentient life. The ruby ray activates the first secret
ray and ultimately all five secret rays. It is the ruby fire of ultimate love that
annihilates ignorance and evil.

CHAPTER 13

1.   The *skandhas* are the transitory elements that constitute our personality
in the realm of time and space. They are form, feeling, ideation, reaction and
consciousness.

2.   The solar disc is an attribute of the Dhyani Buddha Vairochana, whose
name means "he who is like the sun." He conveys all-pervading wisdom, which
is considered the original and consummate wisdom of all the Dhyani Buddhas.

CHAPTER 14

1.   To read the complete story of the Zen teaching on the ox herder, see
D. T. Suzuki's *Manual of Zen Buddhism* (New York: Grove Press, 1960), pp.
127–44; and Paul Reps, comp., *Zen Flesh, Zen Bones* (Garden City, N.Y.: Anchor
Books, Doubleday and Company, n.d.), pp. 131–55.

2.   Soothill and Hodous, *Dictionary of Chinese Buddhist Terms*, p. 47a.

3.   In the original text for this book, which was published in 1975, Gautama
Buddha said in the final chapter: "When the twelve disciples standing as coordinates on the circle, coordinates of the Lord of All the World, have pursued,
like Sumedha, the Ten Perfections of the Law, I will come again to release the
second tier of my instruction in the law of the Buddha and the Mother."